SIMPLY PUT

Practical Biblical Application for all our Life

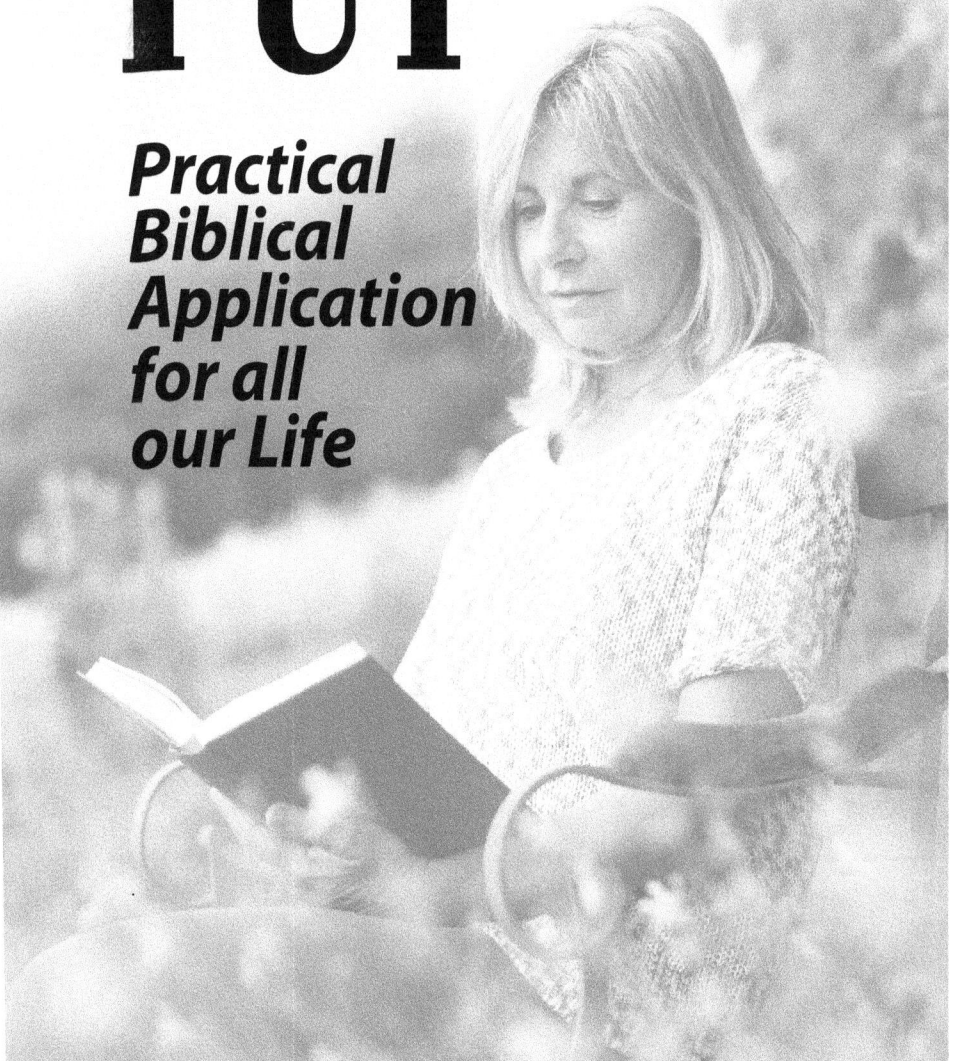

SIMPLY PUT

Practical Biblical Application for all our Life

THERESA J. ROYAL

Hunter Heart Publishing
Colorado Springs, Colorado

Simply Put: Practical Biblical Application For All Our Life
Copyright © 2016 by Theresa J. Royal
First Edition: September 2016

To order products, or for any other correspondence:

Hunter Entertainment Network
4164 Austin Bluffs Parkway, Suite 214
Colorado Springs, Colorado 80918
www.hunter-entertainment.com
Tel. (253) 906-2160 – Fax: (719) 528-6359
E-mail: contact@hunter-entertainment.com
Or reach us on Facebook at: Hunter Entertainment Network
"Offering God's Heart to a Dying World"

This book and all other Hunter Entertainment Network™ Hunter Heart Publishing™, Eagles Wings Press™ and Hunter Heart Kids™ books are available at Christian bookstores and distributors worldwide.

Chief Editor: Gord Dormer
Book cover design: Phil Coles Independent Design
Layout & logos: Exousia Marketing Group www.exousiamg.com
ISBN: 978-1-937741-42-6
Printed in the United States of America.

In Memory of My Beloved Husband Jim Royal

Born March 17, 1933

Went home to be with the Lord

February 13, 2016

Acknowledgments

Thanks to my many friends who helped me bring this book to fruition. I am not even moderately computer savvy, so I needed to get help along the way, especially getting it ready to publish. Special thanks to Eldon Martin and Kay Signer for their computer knowledge; without it, I would not have gotten this to the publisher. Lisa, Eldon's wife, was always there with him to give her advice.

Laurie Pebley helped me with putting the book together chronologically. John Fuson made the picture possible. I thank my Sunday school class and other friends who lifted me up in prayer throughout the process. Tom Schryver helped me understand what was needed to finish this process.

Most of all, my thanks go to my husband Jim who truly used his life for the Lord. It is through him that I found my Savior and Lord, without which I would never have had anything to write about. He encouraged me and even in his dying moments, told me to finish this book.

"as His divine power has given to us *all things that pertain to life and godliness*, through the knowledge of Him who called us by glory and virtue,"
~2 Peter 1:3

Table of Contents

Introduction

Often, when a person reads the Bible for the first time, they are awestruck like I was when I first had one in my hands. You see, I had never actually seen a Bible until I met my husband. Don't get me wrong, I was raised to love and obey God and for that, I am extremely thankful. My birth mother died when I was 18 months old. I was sent by my father to his sister's home for care, as he couldn't do that and continue working. I really remember little of that part of my life. But, I remember quite clearly my Dad, with his new wife, coming from Massachusetts to Philadelphia, Pa. to pick me up at four years old.

My new mom, the only one I remember, was a wonderful mother, and had a most caring and servant spirit. She saw that I went to a good Catholic school until I begged to go to a public high school with my friends, where I later graduated from. My father was one of those good men, so honest that he would drive twenty-five miles to give a dollar back, because he later found they had given him too much change in a transaction. He never went to church, except for weddings and funerals, but he brought us up to have impeccable morals. He promised my mother at their wedding he would bring up any children, including me, in the Catholic faith. This he did, with great commitment.

No two people could be any more different than my husband and I when we started our married life. He was in the Air Force at the time I met him, and had been raised in the Deep South, in the state of Georgia. Coming from two different cultures was enough, but his having been a dyed in the wool Southern Baptist on top of that, sure made us quite a pair. We didn't even eat the same types of food. The only thing we had in common, at the time, was we both loved the outdoors. God certainly used these differences in our married life as the proverbial "heavenly sandpaper."

The young married Sunday school class was a real eye-opener to me. Everyone had a Bible; everyone looked up verses, and knew the Bible, but me. I couldn't tell you where one book was, much less a verse. Oh, I knew all about the Catholic religion, but the Bible might as well have been written in Japanese. To tell you of the years of struggle I went through learning, re-learning, doubting, fearing, meditating, praying, and experiencing truths would take more time and paper than this book could hold.

Caring For Our Children

One thing that has been characteristically true of parents is that they love and are concerned about their children. Even though we know there are some exceptions, I personally thought for years that love and nurturing was an inborn instinct in every mother. I have since found that isn't true.

In the society we live in today, more than ever, parents are concerned about providing for their children. Today, more than ever, children are being over provided for, if anything. They lack for nothing materially. Their parents have degrees from universities that have equipped them well for the great jobs and great salaries they have prepared for. They live in beautiful homes, and have more food than other generations before them. The side effect of this is a new problem, obese children. They go to great schools with endless opportunities for going to an elite university or college of their choice. Yet, they are full of insecurities.

But, wait a minute! Let's look at what they also have to their detriment. They have their own computers, where they can come in contact with every form of pervert that wants to contact them. They can bring up porn sites that they have been given the address for, while Mom and Dad are sleeping. Once, I had a message on my email that I didn't recognize. It said something about Snow White and the Seven Dwarfs. I brought it up, thinking I might save it for the great- grandchildren when they visited. I found out it was one of these hidden porn sights. It just about made me sick to think how some sweet innocent child might think this was alright for them to see.

They have smart phones that allow them to not only keep in contact with their friends through texting every hour of the day, but they can watch video games on demand, spending valuable hours on end. They are actually losing their ability to communicate without the aid of electronic devices.

Once taking our great-grandchild to the Museum of Natural History in Denver, Colorado, we saw a family of four sitting on a bench provided to sit upon and ponder the beautiful scene of Africa encased in glass before them. Were they enraptured by the scene before them? No! They were all glued to their phones, texting. This says it all doesn't it?

But, wait a minute. Let's look what they don't have, that we had (Remember I am 78 years old.) Our parents were equally concerned about us. Some couldn't provide for all our needs like they wanted to, but they saw to it that our most important needs were met. We had their undivided love. Mom was at home daily to love us and teach us the important lessons of life, like good vs. evil, those characteristic traits which would carry us through life and how to treat friends, family, and people in general. Dad came home every evening and was welcomed with hugs and kisses, yells of "Daddy, Daddy!" from the children. Mom had such wonderful meals on the table. She especially loved to fix Dad's favorite where we could see the appreciation written all over his face.

We were taught table manners during meals. Mom sent us to bed early, as we had to get up fresh to go to school the next day. They never did that though until Mom or Dad read bedtime stories to us. How we loved those times. We couldn't watch T.V., because we didn't have any. If we snuck a book under the covers to read, we had to have a flashlight, as our door remained open. Children weren't worried about much in those days; if there was a problem, our parents dealt with them when we weren't around.

Consequently, we were very secure. Those were happy days filled with school, play, and church.

When children started school, they were aware not everyone lived in the same circumstances. Some had much, some very little. But we were taught that Jesus loved all the little children. At this age, we weren't interested in further education. We were too busy running free all over our little town, and playing with all our friends. What freedom we had. Our parents talked to us at home how they couldn't be with us at all times, but God watched us for them and He saw everything we did, and heard everything we said. Since I went to a Catholic School, I was taught morals from the beginning. The wonderful thing was that school, home, and society in general all agreed about what was right and what was wrong.

We all had chores. At home, we had to keep our rooms clean, do the dishes, or take out the trash. Outside, since I had only one sister and no brothers, I had to shovel the snow, wash the car, and WEED the garden, which I hated. By high school, we had already been taught good work ethics, responsibility, accountability, and we knew we didn't get everything we wanted. Those teenage years were when we really learned frugality. They knew we needed to start thinking about what work we wanted to do in life. And we were taught to never go by how much money we would make. Our main consideration should be would we be happy and able to support ourselves and a family. We knew there were certain professions, like a doctor, that would mean we would need further education. But we should do that only if it was a desire to help people. If that was the case, grades were very important, and we would have to earn scholarships and save money ourselves. We could not count on our parents doing it all. Parents guided them to find out where their capabilities and interest lay. The one thing I will never forget was how we were told the most important thing was that we did the very best we could and had integrity, above all else.

Spirituality was not an afterthought with parents in those days. They knew if we didn't love the Lord and please Him, we would never be all we could be. Church was never an option in our house. Though my Dad never went to church, except for weddings and funerals, he never failed to lift up God's ideal to us. As a pastor's wife, I saw a time when families went to church together, then a generation came that sent the children or put them on a church bus.

Then, I saw the most awful thing of all. Church doesn't mean anything at all to some people and they don't even want their children to go. Youth, and children's departments in many churches are dying. Our churches are filled with white hairs. When they die, so will the churches, unless we get back to doing what my family did and teach our children to do it and pass it on, heaven help us. There will be some very hard times ahead of us. We have already seen the beginning of the result of these kinds of homes. Proverbs 22:6 NKJV: "Train up a child in the way he should go, and when he is old he will not depart from it."

Christians Are Losing Their Credibility

How sad it is to me to look around our town, read the newspaper, or watch T.V. and see how we who represent Christ are literally hated around the world. It brings grief and seems like while we weren't looking, it suddenly happened. But, we know this isn't so.

When my husband Jim retired from pastoring and we went to Mexico for eleven years, we were confronted with questions from Christians that were Mexican. Some of the common questions were: "We see you don't live this way, but why are your people, who live in the U.S.A., so immoral?" "Why are you so consumed with sex?" "Why does your country have so many sexual predators?" "Why are there so many divorces?" "Why do so many people take drugs?" etc., etc.

Seriously, I was ashamed and sickened when I was asked these questions. These came from honest, open hearts. They couldn't understand these things. I asked them where they got this distorted view from. Of course, the first thing mentioned was from T.V. or radio. It is unfortunate that many, though extremely poor, have access to this media. If they don't own a T.V. themselves, and many do not, they watch it at family or friend's house. You see, most bring the T.V. outdoors due to the very small, sub-standard houses they live in, in most small villages. All I could do was tell them this depiction wasn't really a true portrayal of the U.S.A. The majority of our country didn't live that way. This was a small minority of the U.S.A.

I am afraid that since the past ten years, this depiction is becoming more accurate. It could be said of us, what is written in Matthew 15:8, NKJV: "These people draw near to Me with their mouth, and honor Me with their lips, but their heart is far from me." Our worship is in vain. We are only following rules taught by men. Since that time, Colorado has legalized same-sex marriages and the legal use of marijuana, medical as well as recreational. The sad situation is that we can't run from it, because it soon will be the whole country that accepts it. Many of the senior Americans who live in foreign countries for retirement are heavy drinkers; live immoral lives, take drugs, and heaven forbid are even shacked up together. No wonder we are losing our credibility, because they tell others that they are Christians.

We came home in the hottest part of summer, each year, so we didn't realize how widespread this had become until then. We were sort of isolated in our small town, which hadn't progressed as quickly as the rest of our country. When we did move back permanently, we were faced with the deterioration of our nation. And the biggest thing we noticed was the loss of credibility of the church. Christian churches of all denominations had lost memberships. Our small town churches had ran around 125-300 congregations, now they were as low as 25-50. Since then, the impact has become greater. One Baptist church in our town has actually become an Art Council, where they give artist lessons.

People's perception of the church is that they are nothing but hypocrites, unloving people there, and churches are not needed anymore. Laws are being made in our country that strips away all our religious freedoms and no one does a thing about it. They totally ignore our

Constitution, and our forefathers' protections within it. I would have a hard time if I had to home school my three sons, but I guarantee I would have done it today. Our schools have become institutions to corrupt the minds of our children. It is not by chance that even children who have been brought up in the church are living worldly lifestyles, and it no longer bothers them.

As Jim and I look at our country today, knowing what we do, we wonder how long before the Lord steps in, and strips us of all our self-reliance. How long before He reduces our mighty power to weakness, and our financial and medical prosperity to poverty and failure. We are rapidly headed that way, and that is how and when God has punished His children in the past.

It is time for America to wake up and realize we are desperately in need of repentance and revival. Stand up U.S.A. and be the Christian nation our forefathers fought for. We need no *secret servants*. What we need is to go back to our churches, and return to being loving, even loving the unlovable. We need to say what we mean and mean what we say. We need to live what we believe. Bury all bigotry, whether racial, financial, educational, social, etc. Refuse to be silent of Whom we believe in. Don't let liberal society direct us, but our Lord, before it is too late and all our freedoms have been removed.

Come in Simple Childlike Faith, That Doesn't Take Proof

How many times have I heard, "If you can prove God exists to me, then, I will believe." You can prove what the Bible says is truth, but really you cannot make a person believe in it. One must have an honest heart, and want down deep to know what it says. Then, that person must come to the Lord in child-like faith.

Yes, I can tell you how faith in God has helped me live the most supernatural life, but all this happened after I first believed. It isn't difficult, that is why the Lord said we must come as a little child. You see, faith is simply believing there is a God, who sent His Son to pay the penalty of sin for people. No matter who that person is, that one couldn't live a good enough life to earn salvation. He did this because He loves us. John 3:16says, "For God so loved the world, that He gave His only begotten Son, that whosoever believeth in Him, should not perish, but have everlasting life." (KJV) And once you find out just how great that love is, it is easy to come to Him, who has already been drawing you to Him.

In this world today, people are stressing knowledge. But knowledge, without the wisdom to use it, is useless. Have you ever seen a genius, who was no earthly good for but one thing? He couldn't even do little tasks that any child could do. It is like the difference in the man who knows the theory, about a job, but is absolutely incapable of doing the job. It is like hiring a part changer, when you can have an expert natural mechanic.

That is why little boys love super heroes. The simple truth is if you want real power, plug into the Power Source, our God who has unlimited power. There is no greater power, and it is only available through faith. Yet, His Ways are definitely not our ways. Isaiah 55:8-9 NKJV says, "For My thoughts are not your thoughts, nor are your ways My ways says the Lord. For as the heavens are higher than the earth, so are My ways higher than your ways, and My thoughts than your thoughts." In fact, they are just the opposite of the world's way. One way is being a servant, rather than being served.

Being last, rather than first, isn't very appealing to our prideful, ambitious, achieving minds. That is the real reason many folk do not believe. If they do, there will have to be some changes made. We have to reason this whole matter out and it involves entering into a moral life with some definite *holy no's*. Wow! Who wants that? Not many people. Who wants accountability, rules, and simply being a good person? The world in general is trying to silence us, so they can appeal to the sensual side of each of us. Not many even want to hear the truth today. If you have an honest, open heart for truth, ask God to show it to you. I can tell you, He will. I don't know how, for it is different for different people. God has never rejected anyone who sincerely wanted to know truth. He will show you He is real. The secret is the honest, open heart. Jesus said once, that even if one was to come back from the dead, they wouldn't believe. How true, some did, they would not believe, and when Jesus arose and walked this earth for forty days, there still were many who did not believe. You see, it wasn't really proof they wanted, no matter what they said. He had fulfilled all scripture, done mighty miracles, and even had eye-witnesses to prove He died and was resurrected.

Knowledge has its place. But let me put it as simple as I know how. Belief in God is a matter of the heart. It changes lives. God can use your knowledge, but let's make one thing clear, He does not need it. He is sufficient. If you remember in Acts 4:7-13 NKJV (Read) when Peter preached before the Sanhedrin, the rulers, elders, and teachers of the law, they couldn't understand how simple, uneducated men could do what miracles they did, and speak like they did. Simply put, they had been with Jesus.

Both men, with degrees, and without degrees, are equally sufficient if they walk with Jesus. It is all of God. He is the source of power through His Holy Spirit.

Doubts

There are a few things I have learned in my 78 years walking on this earth with my Lord. Doubts will come in a Christian's life, and they are normal. God doesn't get angry because we have honest doubts. Doubts can be stepping stones to the other side of spiritual growth. Satan sends doubts to us to get us to stumble in our faith. God uses them to take us to a deeper level of faith.

Don't fear honest doubts. God is able to accomplish what His purposes are for you and your life. And you can be sure that He has a purpose for your life. (Psalm 139:13-18, I Thessalonians 5:24) God does set some up and others down. (Psalm 75:6-7) He doesn't expect us all to be the same. He wants us to be that which He has called us to be, whatever that is. The best job to have is the one God has planned for us to have. The very best place to be is in the center of God's will. I can tell you, the surprise of your life might be God putting you where you cannot even imagine was possible. Ephesians 3:20 NKJV says, "Now to Him who is able to do exceedingly abundantly above all that we ask or think, according to the power that works in us, to Him be glory in the church by Christ Jesus to all generations, forever and ever. Amen."

Probably one of the greatest shocks of my life was when the Lord told me that He could use me to be a pastor's wife. Though neither my husband nor I had any college or seminary training, God made it very clear He wanted us to just surrender to the call and He would do the rest for us, which He did.

As I look back at the twenty-five of Jim's ministry as pastor and mine as his wife and a Bible Study teacher, it boggles my mind as to what He did. After Jim retired in 1995, we went and lived in Mexico and did volunteer mission work for eleven years. Up until last Sunday, Jim is still preaching, filling the pulpit when pastors are on vacation or churches are without a pastor. How old is Jim, well he is 82, as of last March. I still teach a Ladies Sunday school class and a Neighborhood Ladies Bible, yes at 78 years of age. Why am I ever surprised? Jeremiah 32:27 (NKJV) is still in the Bible. "Behold, I am the LORD, the God of all flesh, is there anything too hard for Me?"

Why did I ever have a doubt? Probably the normal, I thought it somehow depended on my abilities, when all He wanted was my availability. Despite any doubts I ever had along the way, God used them to bring me where I am today. The reason I am writing this little book is to let everyone who reads it to know what a great God we have. Why we should never doubt Him. Somehow, through my walk with God, I want to let others know just what He can do with a "nobody". Think it over; no matter who or what you are, He can use you. Be ready for the impossible if He should call. Philippians 4:13 NKJV says, "I can do all things through Christ who strengthens me."

Fantasy vs. Reality

When in Mexico, I learned much from the villages I visited. Not only did I improve on the Spanish I knew, but so much more. Once when I was helping the Mexican children workers of Viva Mexico, (name of a village) to plan and prepare their Sunday school lessons, one lady asked me a question. She wanted to know why I always referred to accounts in the Bible as cuentos, (stories) and not historia (history). I had to think about that, for I didn't know there was a difference. She explained to me in Spanish, as she knew no English, that there was a vast difference. Children were told stories, fantasies, in other words fiction (ficcion), but the Bible was history, not fantasy. I told her in the U.S.A, we simply called them stories.

Well, this was like a light that came on, and I understood clearly what she was telling me. The Bible is *reality*, not fantasy. I know our English language is abused, and definitely not as descriptive as it could be at times, like how we use the word love. But, I had never thought of this before. Could this be one of the reasons our children consider the Bible a myth, not truth? They are told stories from it as well as from Aesop's fables, Dr. Seuss, and others. From the time a child in a Christian home can understand in Mexico, they are told the difference between stories and history, it is fantasy not reality. Never is there a doubt in their minds between the two accounts.

Now, we know there is much more in our world to confuse our children, such as compromise amongst adults, peer pressure, and the propaganda promoted in our schools. But added to the other, this hinders their understanding. This was a lesson I needed to learn and I'll never forget it, and I told that wonderful Mexican lady that day and thanked her.

The Mexican Christians were very committed. The ones we met were not fence riders. I've had quite a few who asked why many of the Americans who went to the American Community Church also drank much alcohol, chain smoked, and attended the American Social Club parties. I told them that many religious groups didn't frown on these things. These people gave testimony that they were Christians, yet they lived the same as non-Christians.

They asked why my husband and I didn't do these things then. I told them it was a personal conviction that many others did not share. They simply could not understand these things, as when they gave their life to the Lord, they didn't want to even give a hint of the old life to confuse others. To them, life was black, or white, there were just no grey areas. Perhaps if it was so with all of us, our children would have less confusion. Read 1 Corinthians 10:31 NKJV: "Therefore, whether you eat or drink, or whatever you do, do all for the glory of God."

We are not islands, standing alone in an open sea. Everyone we come in contact with is looking at our lives, whether we know it or not. What people see tells the story of our relationship with Jesus Christ. I pray that while we were in Mexico those eleven years, people will believe that Jesus Christ does make a difference when He comes into a life, and you can see it. The world's opinion of the U.S.A. is changing, and not for the good. I pray we will realize that so much is at stake. Mexicans I found out love and respect us and many try to copy our lives. Let us realize people are watching us all over the world today.

God is Omnipotent

Simply put, God has UNLIMITED POWER. He is ALL POWER, ALMIGHTY. What great men would give for such power? Yet, God through Christ gifts each of His children with it. He is our Power Source. He alone chooses how much to give each child, according the His purpose for each life.

God loves to take a *nobody*, and make a *somebody* special to cause awe in those who know there is no way these people could do the impossible without God doing it through them. He has done this often, by raising up an uneducated, incapable man to preach mightily and grow a church into a strong witness in a community. Yet, a man who has many degrees ends up an utter failure. The common denominator when this happens is that God just wanted to show that degrees never made a preacher. The Lord does. After seeing this phenomenal ability, the overly qualified man realizes where the Power is. He recognizes His need for God's power and humbly repents. Then, and only then, can God use him. What a difference that makes in a ministry.

Recently, I read two books about Dr. Ben Carson. He is a tremendous example of how God can reach down and touch a man who had no chance in the world to become famous. Yet, because of a mother who had a deep faith in God, and was committed to raise her sons in a hopeless situation with God's help, he went from a victim to a pediatric brain surgeon. He earned fame, fortune, and renown. Though African American, and seen by many as one that would have given up, he rather rose above the poverty, and criminal elements all around him, to help a world that needed his expertise so badly. At the time of this writing, Dr. Ben Carson is running for president. Many say that he hasn't any experience, and cannot make a good president without former political training. Well I don't know what will happen, but I know the same God that raised him from the slums and made him a great surgeon can also guide him to be all that a man must be to be a great president. For after all, God gave him a great mind, gave him wisdom, and he loves to make a man whom no one thinks can do something to be somebody who can do anything God wants to do. Philippians 4:13 NIV (emphasis) says, "I can do **all things** through Christ who strengthens me." Ben's mom believed these words, and so do I. My one prayer is that God would give us a godly president. For, if a man cannot get a word from God in the serious matters facing this nation, we are destined to failure.

Maybe you think you are a supermom. Then, all hell breaks loose and you come to the end of your ropes. You recognize what a failure you really are and you turn to God crying, "HELP!" Just what God wanted all the time. Then, He can pick up the pieces and make you into the mom He wants you to be, a real supermom. For you see, He has all the power any of us need.

It is the same with whatever your call in life. Are you a failure, at wits end corner? Good. Now God can take your life and make you into what He wanted all along. When you are there, you find that you are finally fulfilled. The same formula is needed whoever, and whatever, you find your call in life to be. Luke 1:37 (NKJV) says, "For with God nothing will be impossible."

When you think of Jesus, what do you think of? Is it a baby in a manger, a man who loved little children, a tender caring Good Shepherd, a Savior who took your sin to Calvary, a Loving Lord, faithful and true, or One who answers your prayers? He is all of these, that is true, but how many of you think of Him as He is today, an Awesome Risen Lord? Revelation 1:14-15 (NKJV) says, "His head and hair were white like wool, as white as snow, and His eyes like a flame of fire. His feet were like fine brass, as if refined in a furnace, and His voice as the sound of many waters."

John, when at Patmos, was given a vision, and it was so awesome, he fell at Jesus' feet as dead. Our mind cannot comprehend such splendor. In our human form, we relate to Jesus in His humanity, so we think in terms of what He was then. But right now, in His resurrected body, we bow our knees and worship His awesome greatness. Yes, our Savior is Omnipotent; He has in His hands all the power of the universe. What is your need? Simply present it to Jesus, and realize if He doesn't use it, it isn't because He can't. It must be that, for whatever reason, He is working out His good.

Romans 8:28 (NKJV) says, "And we know that all things work together for good to those who love God, to those who are the called according to His purpose."

God is Omniscient

God simply knows everything there is to know, unlimited knowledge. He is all knowing, about everything. That is why Isaiah 55:8-9 is so true. God knows so much and man knows so little that we often assume what is happening by what seems to be. He sees the whole picture all at once, the past, present, and future.

The only present day illustration I can think of is a pro-football game. There is a blimp above filming for T.V. He has a perfect view of the whole football field. Now, I have purchased tickets to attend said football game, pretty costly at that. I am stuck behind two very obese ladies with big hats to fend off the sun. I am so far up in the stands; it is extremely hard for me to tell what is going on. I can barely see, and if by chance I would sneeze hard, I might miss the most important play of the game.

God is like that blimp, since He knows all; I can go to Him for counsel in any matter in this game of life. I am simply too dumb to make major decisions on the little I can see. Oh, I can pay a lot of money to get counsel from another man, but he would have to give it from what he reads, whether from a book or from his life experiences, however limited they are. It is a comfort to simply trust God and know that He knows; He alone sees all, so He can give me the right direction in any circumstance.

You say, "Well I can't see any good coming from this mess." God can see it, and that is enough. All we need is trust in His perfect knowledge.

God not only has perfect knowledge, but we can depend on His perfect love.

If we could ever realize how great our God is, and throw ourselves on Him, we would end up with less struggles, worries, and accept that He only wants what is best for us. We could even trust Him with our adversities and rejoice even in our sufferings. Why? We would know He doesn't let His children suffer needlessly, so He knows best.

I can look back at my life and see clearly how the good and bad were both used by God for my good. Oh, I questioned at times, I kicked and fought a bit, all to no avail. It would have been a whole lot easier if I simply had entrusted all to my Lord. Today, I am 78 years old, and hopefully a whole lot wiser. I do realize He is worthy to guide my life for me. Too bad I didn't learn that lesson a lot earlier.

I wish I could have seen with my spiritual eyes then what I can today. Now it all makes sense to me, and it will more so when I go home. It will be just as my favorite poem says,

The Weaver

My life is but a weaving, between my God and me.
I do not choose the colors, He worketh steadily.
Oft times He weaveth sorrow and I in foolish pride,
Forget He sees the upper, and I the under side.
Not till the loom is silent, and the shuttles cease to fly,
Will God unveil the canvas and show the reason why.
The dark threads are as needful in the Master's skillful hand,
As the gold and the silver in the pattern He has planned.

~Anonymous

My explanation of the Poem:
God has put my whole life together, for He is so good.
I often forget He is in control, and should be.

He has divine purpose for all, even the bad.
At my death, He will reveal all my life,
Why each and every part of it was molding me,
To be all He wanted me to be, for His glory.

God is Omnipresent

If your husband, like mine, happens to have been a lifer, (mine retired after twenty years in the Air Force) you have a few miles on you. Our life was spent here, there, and everywhere. Moving time was just as normal as apple pie.

As long as I can remember, I always believed God was everywhere. That was because my Mom drilled in me from an early age that she might not always be able to see me, but God could. (A comfort to all moms, our children really never forget those things we drill in them, whether they admit it or not.)

The truth of these words is that God was with me in Germany, in Holland, in France, on the island of Guam, in Mexico, and in the many states we lived in. My husband went to many places I didn't go to on his temporary duty stations. He'll gladly testify God was with him, in Northern Africa, Japan, Hong Kong, etc.

What I want you to know for certain is that our God is everywhere, as others who have travelled more than us will tell you. This is so comforting to people, but it is also very stressful to those who have been running from God. No matter where you go to hide, you cannot escape God's love and presence. And don't forget God's promise in Hebrews 13:5, He has promised He will never leave you or forsake you. If you need Him He says, "Draw near to God and He will draw near to you." (Jeremiah 29:13, James 4:8)

In those times that Jim had to be gone from us, God never let me down. He was always there and He met every need I committed to Him and many I failed to commit to Him. I truly don't know how a woman who is married to an active military man can survive without the Lord. No, you are never alone. He is ALWAYS THERE, just waiting for you to come to Him.

Once, while we were stationed in Germany, my son Jamie was diagnosed with a tumor in his right femur. It was decided he needed to be air-evacuated to Walter Reed Hospital right away. Because I needed to be with the other boys in school, and I was way too emotional to deal with the situation, my husband flew to the hospital with Jamie. Communications were in no way like they are today, so I just had to trust God. And I did, and I found He was sufficient even with the broken heart I was dealing with. To make a long story short, it was not a malignant tumor, but one that could have caused him to lose his leg. (The last words he had said to me on leaving was "Don't let them take my leg off, I'd rather die." This didn't help matters at all.)

Of course, I prayed with all my heart while they were gone. And I believe with all my heart that He heard my prayers. When Jamie died of a brain tumor at age fifty-four, the thought entered my mind and I believe God placed it there, that He had given me forty plus grace years with my wonderful son.

I got to see him grow up, graduate from a junior college, marry a wonderful Christian woman, have two wonderful children, and become a strong, yet gentle law enforcement officer for thirty-two years. We even got to go to his retirement service after serving twenty-five years on the Colorado Springs Police Dept. who had already rehired him on the Drop Plan. No mother and father could thank God enough for having that privilege. I will share more on his death in another chapter.

Not only has God been with me at all times in the past, but He has also promised He would never leave *me* or forsake *me*. What a comfort this verse is to a military wife, or a wife who has been left behind when the Lord called her husband home. I often meditate on how my life has changed in these latter years due to age. What a wonderful encouragement to know I will never be alone. My greatest friend will always be near me to guide me. Jim has always done all the business in our family. He is especially good at finances. Yet, I would never have a worry, whatever the case might be. My Guide will be there when no one else is. Jim is always reminding me he has put money aside for my retirement. He tells me not to worry. He and others in our family seem to want to be certain I will be cared for. I don't think they realize just how serene I am about that situation. For my heavenly Father is rich in cattle and land. Why should I have to concern myself with being cared for?

Headlines:
"God Isn't Fixing This!"

Recently, I heard on the news, and saw the picture on the front page of a major newspaper, after another terrorist episode had taken place. In bold letters across the front page were the headlines, "God Isn't Fixing This." One newscaster translated it as "Don't pray, it won't help this." I was riled up, I have to admit, for I realize what they wanted all to know, is our God is too weak, so all our prayers don't matter at all. "Look, it's only getting worse."

Now I, as well as others, realize a few truths about prayer. For one, you cannot ask amiss and think you can move God to do anything you want, no matter what He is doing. Sure, we can ask within His will and He will answer that prayer for He has promised that in Jeremiah 33:3 (NKJV), "Call unto Me and I will answer you, and show you great and mighty things you do not know," But, He also has said so much more about this matter of prayer answering. As I have matured as a Christian, I realize more and more that His sovereign will is of utmost importance. He clearly says His ways are not our ways. Not only does He know what is needed while I only think I do, but I can't begin to understand what He is allowing to happen to wake up the U.S.A.?

We have been blessed so much, the world has longed for what God has given to us. Of utmost importance is our freedoms granted to us in our Constitution. Are we as a grateful nation? When I see protestors in our streets, protesting the very rights our forefathers died for, I cringe. I ask myself, could God be allowing these very rights to be removed, so we can realize how precious they are? Perhaps!

As I looked at the incident in San Bernardino, California, I heard some, including those in the highest level of our government, say that it is because of our gun rights. How can that be, when it happened in our most liberal state, in a gun free zone, where not even one had a gun to defend themselves. Now we are hearing more cries to remove guns. It is so simple. "Guns don't murder people, people using guns and many other weapons, kill people." If we could not protect ourselves, there would be victims of so much more crime. Could God be testing us to see just how much we appreciate all the freedoms and blessings He has given us? Will we appreciate them enough to fight for them? Will we stand and say God hates radical Islamic terrorism, no matter how politically incorrect this is? Yet, this isn't saying in any way, that we hate Muslims. God loves all people. If we are His, we love them too. This isn't saying we will not be vigilant, wise, and committed to protecting our nation. We will do this also.

Our prayers are not in vain. God is listening. Perhaps what is happening is the same as when Daniel prayed in Daniel 10:12-14 (NKJV).God heard and He said He did immediately, but Satan fought strongly and detained the answer. Though delayed, the answer came to Daniel.

Many godly people think we as a nation have become too corrupt. We have left God's will, His Word, His Way and He has already made up His mind not to answer our prayers, because of our rebellion. Jeremiah 7:16 (NKJV) says, "Therefore do not pray for this people, nor lift up a cry or prayer for them, nor make intercession to Me; for I will not hear you."

If it weren't for the fact that our God is so compassionate and merciful, I might agree. But, I cannot overlook this. There is still a remnant of true believers who are committed to fight for this land and what made it such a great nation. We have a great God, and we who know Him intimately know He is always waiting for believers to claim all His precious promises in His Word. 2 Chronicles 7:14 (NKJV) says, "If my people who are called by My name will humble themselves, and pray and seek My face, and turn from their wicked ways, then I will hear from heaven, and will forgive their sin and heal their land." If we do this, He will forgive and heal our land.

Healing is Simply "All of God"

The foundation I must establish before going on is all healing is from God. Even the greatest doctors run into obstacles or cases that are beyond their abilities. Any honest doctor, with any sense at all, realizes they are limited. It is also true that medications are limited, because not all people respond to the same medication, or their bodies can tolerate the same amounts.

Our technological expertise today is remarkable. If anyone needs help today, whether medically, surgically, or with medications, this is the day to live in, especially in the U.S.A. No other country in the world has been so blessed with knowledge, institutions of education, or the prosperity, as we have been. We have some of the greatest minds, but we know who made these men, and their minds. I believe that is why God gave us so many of these men and women. Due to our charitable nature, many from nations around the world have been flown here to be treated. Many of our doctors have done it pro bono, because we also have been given compassionate hearts like no other country in the world.

Whether with doctors or without doctors, with medications or without medications, with the anointment of oil, or without the anointment of oil, with prayer, or without prayer, it matters not. Sometimes, out of God's unlimited grace, He simply heals. He is where the Power is, no matter how gifted man is; it is ultimately all of God.

Oh yes, God expects us to use these availabilities, since He provided them, but don't depend upon them, depend upon God. And sometimes God allows their treatments not to work; simply to show us how great is our God. And, always remember perfect healing also comes from God. It is called death. If you ponder this, it is truly the perfect healing of all for a Christian. That is why the Lord tells us not to grieve like the world does. 1 Thessalonians 4:13 (NKJV) says, 'But I do not want you to be ignorant, brethren, concerning those who have fallen asleep, lest you sorrow as others who have no hope." Why? Because we do have a hope, where others do not, man cannot top God's healing. For the believer, death is total freedom from all the woes of this world, and eternal fellowship with God."

No, God does not heal everyone who asks. If He doesn't, it is for a reason. Just look at the Apostle Paul's life. God, rather than heal his infirmity, showed him that His grace was sufficient in weakness, and His strength was made perfect living in weakness. (2 Corinthians 12:7-10, my version.) Paul's life was a testimony of what God could do through weakness. This is why so many people who suffer the most seem to be so strong. The infirmity has truly brought them to their knees, and there God spoke to them. They were far better used in their weakness.

Hope Deferred

Sometimes, hope is the only thing we have left. No matter what happens in life, however bad the adversity that comes to an individual, as long as there is hope, one can survive, even the greatest tragedies in life.

Hope is what a Christian has that a non-Christian does not have. I know that whatever Satan threw at me in life, God and His precious promises would get me through them. Even when I was a child, though lost, I believed God was real and knew every time I hurt, He succored me to Himself and showed me He loved me. I didn't have a Bible to go to, but I knew He was there and He cared. It got me through the times I felt no one else cared for me.

Added to that knowledge was that there was a tomorrow and what was today would pass and it would get better. Once, a nun in school made a statement that would stay with me, even to this day. She said, "When things get very bad, say, "This too shall pass." And when life couldn't be better say, "This too shall pass." It kept me aware all throughout life that nothing stays as it is today. Like the Bible says, "…for He makes His sun rise on the evil and on the good, and sends rain on the just and on the unjust." (Matthew 5:45, NKJV) What He was saying is that in life, good and bad things happen to both the just and unjust. It simply is life.

There are many myths in life. They are what people think life will be. Sometimes, they are those dreams we have of what we want our life to be.

Dreams are not hope, and they can be destroyed. One of those dreams is we will have a wonderful childhood; we'll meet and wed the most wonderful man. We'll be treated with love and kindness by this man, and we, of course, will have wonderful, obedient children. We will follow God's way so that'll guarantee they will never disappoint us. I may or may not have a career, and of course I will balance home and job perfectly. God will just bless and bless. Like children say today, WRONG!!! If you ever thought this way, I would say you are hallucinating. This is not reality.

You see, we live in a sin-scarred world and Satan is very real. You have taken him completely out of the picture. There is evil in this world. Satan's goal at the very least is to neutralize anything God does, and his goal is to take away all our hope and convince us that God doesn't love us. Like I mentioned in another chapter, there is always someone in every school, home, and job place that constantly stirs up trouble and makes our life difficult. Yet, God says we have to love them despite the difficulty they cause. It is a simply a test to see if we know what God's love is.

God teaches us so much through the difficulties of life that He cannot do otherwise. If all goes well, how would we ever learn true patience, how to suffer long, if someone or some difficulty didn't stretch and stretch our limit to put up with those things? It could be our husband, or a child, a parent, or more likely an in-law.

How is God's forgiveness made perfect in us? By constantly facing a difficult person who needs forgiveness. I learned through teaching V.B.S. that the children who push our buttons the hardest, are only crying out for love and attention. They get our attention by doing bad things if they have to. We can tell children we love them, but when they try your patience over and over again and you *continue* to love them, only then do they believe you. We don't know what is going on in their home. Could they be crying out, "HELP ME!"

Once I was the V.B.S. Director and the teachers were told to bring problems they couldn't handle, to me, so they wouldn't disrupt the class attending to them, their selves. I'll never forget one such time when a teacher had this boy about eight years old by the ear and brought him to me. I told her to go back to class and I would talk with him. It seems he was accused by two sweet little girls of an infraction, and since he was a troubled child, they automatically believed them over this boy.

Upon talking with him, he admitted he got in lots of trouble, but this time, he didn't do what these girls had accused him of. I sent for the girls and had a talk with them. I asked them to please tell me the truth and I promised all that was needed was an apology if they were wrong and how this would hurt him if it wasn't true. They both cried, admitted they had lied, and they truly were sorry. Later, after I talked it over with the teacher, she agreed she had acted on impulse, due to stress.

Well, I made a true friend that day. I'd see this boy at church, and he would give me a big hug. But the best was when years later, I ran into him in Wal-Mart. I hardly recognized him, as he was now a young man and had changed during the years. He told me he had a wonderful family and they were all in church. I don't have to tell you how happy I was for him. Maybe, he was one of those boys who finally found hope, because someone finally stuck up for him. I passed his test of love and patience that day.

In a world with so many hurting souls, we have to be concerned more about today and showing we really love the unlovely, even if it is difficult at times. They need to know God is love, and He loves them. How will they ever have this hope that gets them through life? "That Christ may dwell in your hearts through faith; that you, being rooted and grounded in love, may be able to comprehend with all the saints what is the width, and the length and depth and height-to know the love of Christ which passes knowledge; that you may be filled with all the fullness of God." (Ephesians 3:17-19, NKJV)

There are more people committing suicide today than ever. We know that this is a crisis. Many of them are hopeless. We as Christians, at times, get so caught up with *Last Days Prophecies* that we miss out on *today*. Our world needs love, forgiveness, hope, joy, patience, etc. Only we, who are forgiven, been loved, have joy, and patience can help them. Yes, at times our hope may be deferred, but as long as there is an eternal God, and a Savior who loves us and gave His love by dying on the cross for us, it never can be destroyed.

Ignorance is Bliss

How can people ignore all the dangers to our way of life that is taking place in our world? Can a people live in the age of technology, travel daily on the information highway, and totally ignore the cultural and political destructive plots all around them?

Recently, I had the opportunity to observe firsthand how this happens. I was in a home where they have nothing but local news on T.V. Actually, they do not watch anything but nature documentaries provided by P.B.S. They do not subscribe to the newspapers or magazines where they might find out what is going on in our world or the world in general. Even their newspaper does not cover conservative issues. No one discusses religion, politics, personal opinions, or news. They make it clear that in their home, they will not listen to what they call *negatives*. What we discovered is they have silenced anyone who might say anything that could challenge their Utopian philosophies. The illustration that, like ostriches, they have their heads stuck in the sand is so visibly demonstrated in their lives. They do not want anyone to speak of God or Christ for then, they would recognize their own evil, which they truly believe is good.

Now when I say evil, I do not mean murder, rape, theft, or other criminal actions. No, these people strive to have honorable intentions and actions. They no doubt are the first to give for a medical or benevolent need. They will run miles for a charitable marathon, while at the same time thinking marijuana should be legalized, drink their selves into oblivion, hate what they call "Bible thumpers," and call any true, caring people for the freedoms we fight for "right wing radicals". They elevate obscenities, laugh at homosexuality and true morals, despise those who follow a code of moral discipline, and embrace all who agree with them.

It literally breaks my heart to see the ignorance shared by so many people. To us, the spiritual realm is our very life and the Bible a true road map for life. To the lost, the spiritual realm is the world of demonic counterfeits. They study spirits, but ignore true spirituality and the true God Himself.

How can one possess such zeal for wrong? They have zeal without knowledge. Romans 10:1-3 (NIV) says, "Brothers, my heart's desire and prayer to God for the Israelites is that they may be saved. For I can testify about them that they are zealous for God, but their zeal is not based upon knowledge. Since they did not know the righteousness that comes from God and sought to establish their own, they did not submit to God's righteousness." Yet, they are blinded to the truth. They cannot see truth, and do not want anyone to speak truth where they would have to hear it. Their senses are numb to it. Their hearts are hardened to the truth. I have come to believe that the reason is they cover their eyes and stop up their ears. If they heard and saw truth, they might have to experience a crack in their philosophical belief system and have to leave their present lifestyle, including friends who live by this same lie.

When a police officer is killed, no one says a thing. But let a thug, or rebel, be killed due to an officer feeling if he doesn't shoot, his life will be taken, there will instantly be local agitators to rise up, then, state and national agitators. This can be nothing but a national organized group, who wait for anything to yell about. Our media loves the sensationalism, so they give them all the covering they desire. This is a national perversion of justice. I would be the first to stand for a senseless killing of a black person.

What I cannot tolerate is passing judgment before one has even heard the truth of the matter.

Some of these people, believe it or not, were raised in godly homes where the Bible was taught and God was the center of their home. Their parents lived in a love relationship with God and His Son and it appeared their children would all follow in their footprints. What happened? Are we not seeing a mass departure from the church? Is there not a generational abandonment of the faith? How could this happen? Where does the fault lay? Have their parents failed? Should we blame the schools? Is it cultural? Is it due to the media? Is it our churches? All have a part for sure. It happens little, by little. But, we must remember above all, the guilt falls on the individual who makes a conscious choice to reject truth, and substitute it with a lie. There are many godly people who would love to say what is really going on, but out of fear, they remain silent.

That is why an individual raised in an ungodly home where there is substance abuse, physical and mental abuse, and filth of every imaginable form, leave that world, get saved, give their life completely to the Lord, and become a man or woman after the heart of God. No one ever prayed for them, no one demonstrated godliness to them, yet he or she "chose" to follow God's Will, God's Way, God's Word. It can and does happen. Everyone is truly without excuse. And this doesn't exonerate us from telling the world that Jesus saves. That is our commission.

A good example of this is Dr. Ben Carson, a black boy, who was raised in Detroit where crime is rampant. He had a mother, a single mom, who was determined to see her boys raised in the church. She saw to it that they didn't run wild in the streets. Though she had no education, couldn't even read, she saw to it that her boys got a good education. She worked at night cleaning offices, after working for people all day. What was the end result? She raised two exceptional young men, who broke the barrier of poverty, and climbed out of the ghetto.

I'll Simply Get a Purge

A new product (new to me at least) I've noticed on the market is colon purges. Now, I am aware that some people have lazy bowels and occasionally have to use these products under the guidance of a medical doctor. However, as with everything else, this product, which can be bought off the shelf, is being used or better stated, misused by some.

Among those misusing these products are teens along with diuretics leading to bulimia, and anorexia. The sole purpose is being to keep their weight down. They eat whatever they want, sometimes over-indulging. Then, they get a colon cleanser. We agree that this is a time of life that living in this society demands perfection, especially in weight control.

Spiritually some, living a life of abandonment, fill their life with every form of immorality and lack of restraint. They forsake all limits, controls, and subjection to authority, and live by their own lustful nature. Many live in fantasy land and think they will never be held accountable for their actions. Numbers 32:23b (NKJV) says, "…and be sure your sin will find you out."

After all, they assume they will live a full life of just doing what comes natural. If they do want to change for the better, isn't God a loving God, won't He forgive all? This is not reality, but a lie of the devil. You cannot avoid the scars of sin. It is not as simple as over-indulging on food, going to the drug store to buy a purge, taking it to cleanse your colon, and all the garbage you have put in your body will be purged out.

Once you have played either with drugs, alcohol, sexual deviations, speeding, and risks of all forms, you are **never satisfied**. You think you control whatever it is, but the reality of the matter is that one day, it controls you. You are what we call an *addict*, and crave **more, and more**. This is the end product that you cannot just simply purge away overnight.

Even if you do turn to the Lord, He forgives, He forgets, but you are left with the scars of sin. You will fight against these cravings the rest of your life. These unwanted urges are the areas that Satan will use against you all the days of your life. They will be your areas of vulnerability, or weakness. Yes, you can call on God's power, but you have given Satan an area that will be his greatest weapon against you.

If only a young person could get a glimpse of the struggles they are opening their life to while they could still stop them, I believe they would make better choices. And if they didn't turn to God, oh the pain, the grief, the end would be anything but pretty. I pray some of you, if you are young, will look at this differently. Or if you are a parent, speak to them out of love and give them a glimpse of a man or woman homeless, living from one fix to another, or old, ugly, abused, lying on the street with the garbage. God made you for so much more than that. (Jeremiah 29:11-13, any version.)

David was a man after the heart of God, yet God did not take away the scars of sin. They are the by-product of sin. Oh, God paid the penalty of sin for your soul, but listen to what God told David: 2 Samuel 12:1 says, The child born of David's adultery would die, 2 Samuel 12:14, David's son Amnon raped David's daughter Tamar, 2 Samuel 13:14, His son Absalom murdered Amnon, 2 Samuel 13:13:28-29, Absalom brought the kingdom into rebellion and for the rest of David's reign, there was violence. He knew he was forgiven, but as predicted, "the sword never departed from David's house." (2 Samuel 12:10, NKJV) The simple truth, you cannot just purge out the scars of sin. Build your life upon Jesus Christ and His Will, His Way, and His Word. This is the only way to joy and blessings.

In Times Like These

In 1944, Ruth Caye Jones wrote this song that Jim and I have sung many times, mostly in southern Baptist churches, "In Times Like These."[1] I don't hear it sung much anymore, but the words are more appropriate for these times than ever. The first time I heard it sung was as a duet harmonizing, and I thought it was beautiful. But, I must admit I didn't fully understand the depth of meaning to the words of this song.

When I was a child of around four years old, my uncles went to WWII and were stationed in Europe. I remember the seriousness on the faces of family members. But, I was too young to grasp war. I remember adults worrying when the Korean War broke out. The Vietnam War was clearer in my mind, and I was clearly aware this war divided our country.

As the bride of an Air Force man, I began to realize that he, too, could be called to go to Vietnam, as he was a Forward Air Controller at this time and could be dropped into the jungle with electronic devices to call in planes on targets. All of this, for the first time, brought the reality of the real concern of war. The truth was times were severe, and we heard of

---

[1] Jones, Ruth Caye. "In Times Like These." Sydney: Aberbach (Aust.), ©1944
1 score (3 p.); 28 cm. Copyright 1944 by Mrs. Ruth Caye Jones, copyright assigned 1958 to Zondervan Music Publishers.

many foxhole conversions. Men realized for the first time their need of a Savior, as they faced the strong possibility of being killed.

Still, I never truly knew how powerful the words of this song were until now. Before, we knew clearly who our enemy was. Though some may have disagreed with going to war, they were very patriotic and didn't take freedom lightly. They also knew they were the envy of the world.

Today, we are faced with a different enemy. Some in our land won't even identify who that enemy is. Somehow, they think if they don't speak of them, they will go away. We as a nation are more polarized by politics, race, education, sex, and class than ever. Our country has been weakened for the first time in my life. Every time one goes to a mall, church, school, theatre, or work place, they can never know for sure that some radical Islamist, racist, or deranged person might blow them up. Never did I dream that in my lifetime we would be reduced to this. Never did I ever say in times like this you'd better have a Savior, an anchor, to give you stability during these troubled times.

As I was getting my morning coffee, preparing for my devotion time, this song popped into my mind. I pondered the words of this song and I realized how powerful they were for today. Our leaders can minimize or deny all threats, but they are very real and are everywhere. Not just in the Middle East, or Europe, but here too. We lived in Colorado Springs for about ten years. My son worked for the Police Dept. there for twenty-five years. None of us ever thought any idealist would one day take the lives of many just to make a statement. Our town is a very small town, a peaceful, loving town, but we are not so foolish as to think this horror could not happen here. I don't care who you are, where you are, in times like these, you better be prepared. Part of that preparation is spiritual.

I am prepared. You see, I have an anchor for these times, Jesus, my Savior and Lord. If by some chance this terror comes here, it matters not. I am prepared. I love my family, my church family, and if I live to see my 80's and even 90's, that'll be O.K. But if I die, it is gain, as Paul said. In times like these, I have a Savior, and I am sure my anchor holds and grips the Solid Rock.

It's Simply All of God

It took me years to realize this simple, but profound truth. Theoretically, if someone asked me if I could do anything in my own power, I would have said NO. However, it didn't all click together for years that whatever I did, I had to throw myself upon Christ and His Holy Spirit for power. He was and is my Power Source.

I imagine I didn't have a full understanding of just how amazing His sustaining grace is. 2 Corinthians 12:9 (NKJV) says, "My grace is sufficient for you, for My strength is made perfect in weakness." His grace is anything I cannot do for myself, but only God can do through me. To try to make anything happen on my own is futile. Whether it is in the role of a wife, mother, job, or the Lord's work, it doesn't matter. Somewhere along life's path, we discover we are an utter failure without Him. Even if our goals are well-meaning, it still doesn't matter.

One of the myths of life is if we marry, we will live happily ever after. That probably comes from all the fairy tales our parents read to us as little children and the narrow vision we had in the Lord's promises, that if we just did right, all would be just glorious all the time.

How can two people who come from two completely different cultures, religions, diets, political backgrounds, families, etc. never have a difference in opinions? Take my husband and I, we are perfect examples.

Jim was raised in the Deep South, and I in New England. That alone, was enough to cause much friction. I had a more rigid upbringing; my parents sheltered their two girls. My husband simply ran free in the country of Egypt, Georgia. He lived along the Ogeechee River with the poisonous snakes, and had his own shotgun early in life. He accepted the Lord as a small child in a Southern Baptist Church in Egypt.

I went to a Catholic school for the first eight years of school (we had no kindergarten then) and was deeply trained in the teachings of the Catholic Church. I knew much about the Lord, but I knew nothing about developing an intimate relationship with Him. That we were totally different is an under-statement. We didn't even eat the same type of foods. My Mom never deep fried anything, not even chicken. Jim's family deep fried everything, chicken, fish, even vegetables. Though I had been taught how to cook from an early age, my husband said I didn't know how to cook very well, as I didn't cook like they did in Georgia. I'd never seen grits, greens soaked in grease, fried okra, hush puppies, and never had eaten biscuits and gravy, squirrel brains, or catfish stew.

I loved art, music, creativity, and school and he loved hunting, fishing, and guns, and taught our boys to do the same. Though my dad loved to hunt and fish, I had never seen a real gun in our home. He must have kept them at his friend's house. Jim was a firm believer that if you taught your boys how to use a gun right when they were young, they would treat it right and never get hurt.

My family raised their girls totally different than his parents did. When my boys were growing up, I wondered what I was doing wrong, for as our home in Massachusetts was always quiet with just two girls, seven years apart in age. My boys were rambunctious, active, and picked on each other constantly. Jim was a strong disciplinarian, whereas my dad was firm, but we hardly ever received corporal punishment. He was more of a privilege remover. If my sister and I disagreed, I can't remember it. She says she sometimes wished I would take her with me when I told my mom I didn't want to. She was so good she hardly ever needed discipline. I guess the only thing Jim and I had in common was we were very verbal, or opinionated. I really believed another myth. If parents raised children right and saw they were raised in the Lord, they'd always choose right. WOW! What a rude awakening.

Because Jim and I wanted a solid home dedicated to the Lord, we worked out all the differences as the years passed. We truly were heavenly sand paper, sanding out all the rough spots in each other. But we still had and still have different ideas and only the Lord and dedicated love to God and each other kept us, and still today keep us together. Our love has remained strong despite differences.

Just imagine a Massachusetts born gal, raised to be an independent thinker, very verbal woman, married to a Georgia guy who was raised to believe every woman should be silent and in her place, totally under the control of her husband. I guess the Lord has a great sense of humor putting the two of us together. The fact is that as the years have passed, He has made us into two well-rounded individuals that are truly one flesh. And the effect this has had on our children, adding the fact they moved around the world for twenty years, has been phenomenal. They are truly unique individuals, loving, caring for all people, very flexible, totally unbiased, and have taken the best of their Mom and Dad.

We lost one son to a brain tumor, but we found out at the funeral that he had touched unlimited numbers of people's lives, and was loved by all. The Chief of Police told the group at his retirement ceremony that he even got letters from people who had gotten tickets from Jamie, saying what a fine young man he was, and he did the right thing. The two left are still capable of failures, like Jamie was, and are not entirely what the Lord wants them to be, like us; He's not finished with them either.

I pray daily for all my family members, church needs, our pastor, my Sunday school class and all others I know that have needs. I believe that is where the power is. I will do this until I go home to be with the Lord. Each of them is different, each has different needs, different weaknesses, strengths, and yet each is a soul loved by God and loved by me. Yet, I know if anything happens, it will be all of God.

Just Give Me the Simple Life

Have you ever heard this phrase? Life, if you think about it, is anything but simple. That is unless you have learned the secret that God is the Problem Solver. If you have reached the maturity in your Christian life where you have learned to place **all** in God's hands immediately, you have learned a well-kept secret. You didn't struggle with problems and adversities, until you finally came to your senses and remembered verses like Jeremiah 32:27: "I am the Lord, the God of all flesh, is there anything too hard for me?" and "For with God nothing will be impossible." (Luke 1:37) Then, you placed them into Jesus' hands and wondered why you didn't do that in the first place.

Aren't we foolish to carry burdens ourselves that He promised to carry for us? Why do we do it over and over again? We never seem to learn from our mistakes. The chorus from the Christian Hymn 'Tis So Sweet To Trust in Jesus" says it all, words written by Louisa M.R. Stead[2]:

Jesus, Jesus, how I trust Him!

How I've proved Him o'er and o'er!

---

[2] Stead, Louisa M.R. "Tis So Sweet To Trust in Jesus." Music by William J. Kirkpatrick. Written in 1882, Louisa M.R. Stead. *Songs of Triumph.*

Jesus, Jesus, precious Jesus!
O for grace to trust Him more and more!

Burdens are lifted when we go to the Great Problem Solver, and let Him carry them for us. If we would do that, He would be faithful to carry them for us, or make them ever so light. Matthew11:28-30, NKJV says, "Come to Me, all you who labor and are heavy laden, and I will give you rest. Take My yoke upon you and learn from Me, for I am gentle and lowly in heart, and you will find rest for your souls. For My yoke is easy and my burden is light."

It matters not if it is your family, your job, your circumstances, your health, your happiness, the world situations, your church, or others. You can never have peace until you lay them all at the feet of Jesus. Let go, and let God work it out. And whatever you do, do not pick it up again. To do so would to be saying I can handle it better, and that is not the "Good Life". It is rather a life of confusion and misery, a life of dealing with Satan's attacks every day.

Yes, give me the simple life. It only comes from trusting Jesus with all things, great and small. We are the ones who make them big. I have to admit I still have a problem with this. But, when I practice what I teach, I enter into the peace that passes understanding. Give me grace to trust You more.

Mothers & Sons

Being raised in a quiet home of just two girls who were seven years apart, to say it was an adventure raising three boys, is putting it mildly. Sometimes, it was more like being on a trip, so to speak. My three sons were quite different in personality, which I gather is quite normal for brothers.

Bob, the oldest, was the only one you could call an achiever in school. He got good grades, and loved pleasing people. He was outgoing, made friends easily, and never minded moving as often as we did with Jim in the Air Force. He always adapted very easily when changing schools and moving to a new neighborhood. He wasn't one to get in trouble, but we found out as years went on, that he liked to instigate it. He never participated in any sports, as he had a gentle spirit.

Our middle son was the dynamo of the three. He was very energetic and would love to take on any dare. He never was very interested in school and barely was promoted each year. Not that he was dumb, far from it; he was more of a class clown. He re-did kindergarten, as the teacher as well as we thought he couldn't keep up. Later, we realized he was just never interested.

From about five years old, he said he wanted to grow up and be a cop, and though that was a common goal of most little boys, he never changed his mind. He went on to Jr. College, majored in Police Science and excelled all the way through. He even had a 4.0 average one semester. He had a charming personality and could get out of much trouble just by putting on that smile. It really came in handy when he became a police officer. He was very dedicated and loved his work.

Jeff, our youngest, was quite a different child. He was a very quiet child. He came along four years later than the middle child, and loved his big brothers. I think they welcomed him, as there was always sibling rivalry between the oldest two boys. I hardly knew he was around when the older boys were in school. He was a true introvert.

The one problem he had that made life difficult for us was that he hated school. I mean, really, he hated it. He was extremely smart, but he never would try to achieve. I literally had to push him out the door many times, both of us crying as he begged to stay home. He hated to move from place to place, as he hated change. He did not adjust easily to any type of change. He always loved music, and finally joined the band and played the trumpet when he was in Jr. High. He never cared to join any sports.

I don't know how the U.S. Navy did it, but years later after a long cruise at sea, he came home and talked more in one hour than I think he ever did in his whole life. We couldn't believe the change. He simply told us you couldn't be an introvert on a destroyer at sea.

When my three sons were teenagers, I had a hard time controlling them. By then, Jim was working at NORAD in Colorado Springs, his last tour in the Air Force, and he worked shift work. Since he was gone a lot, the boys really didn't listen to me. I was part of the reason, as I hated to spank them. I was too tender-hearted. They really challenged my authority and would just laugh at me when I threatened them. Jeff was still pretty young and didn't get into much trouble, at that time. I had to stay on my toes, as Jamie was always in trouble at school. I wondered if he really would be a cop or join the robbers. But down deep, he was really the most conscientious of the three.

When my husband had to discipline them, I would go in the bedroom and cry. This way they couldn't see me, or they would have an ally, and Jim knew it. Later when grown, they shared they never got enough discipline, even though I thought they got too much. But they never resented the years Jim believed in not sparing the rod. In fact, these three sons have loved their Dad and Mom till this day and have shown us in many ways. Before Jamie died, he told his Dad that he was more than a father, he was his best friend. At this time, we had moved to Mexico and he missed us. And he was the boy who got the most spankings of all.

Years later when my youngest son was in Bible school in Memphis, Tennessee, we got to go to Adrian Roger's church, Bellevue Baptist, for a conference. One of the classes I and my daughter-in-law attended was on mothers and their sons (they had two sons.) What an eye opener that was. The leader said one reason boys don't want to obey their mothers was because they were males, and rejected a woman ruling over them. I sure could relate to that. They fight to the end for that reason. Finally, since they have grown, they realize for the first time Mom only wanted the best for them. Jim was definitely Justice, and I was definitely Mercy. My middle son and his wife bought me a picture and it said, "There is a special place in heaven for the mother of three boys." That summed it up very well.

It is never an easy task to raise three sons, but I assure you that God's grace is sufficient. Looking back, the benefits far outweigh the difficulties. It is amazing to see them as adults, and realize just how great they are. Oh, they definitely are not perfect, but they have such kind hearts and sweet spirits. We must have done something right. God still knows best, and the closer we follow His will, the more we reap the benefits. God's ways are still better than the world's ways.

If you are the mother of girls, you have different problems. They are usually very emotional, which brings a different type of struggle. When you get to my age, you realize it was definitely some of the best days of your life having them at home. One day they are gone, but they soon bring home grandchildren. Of course, they are perfect in every way. I never thought I could ever love my great-grandchildren as much as I did their parents when they were young. How wrong I was. I absolutely love them, and am thankful for each one.

Since I wrote this chapter, my husband died of cancer. I cannot tell you how my two sons were there for me during this time. Dad hung on till the last family came home, and he died at home with his family. As soon as the grandchildren and boys, with wives and my deceased son's wife and grown children were all home, he died. They were such help. I now know why God gave me those boys. They have loved me and met every need I could possibly have. Not only that, but they told me they would always be there for me. They meant it, and it has been a great comfort.

READ EACH VERSE IN THE BIBLE

My favorite chapter in the Bible: Psalm 91

My favorite verse: 2 Timothy 1:12b. I did the committing, He does the keeping.

My favorite promise: Jeremiah 32:27:Absolutely nothing is impossible with God, for He is the God of all flesh.

My verse why I teach: Ezra 7:10, Acts 22:14-15: God has called me to let Him teach through me. I have dedicated my life to let Him do it. It is actually all of Him.

My knowledge of Jesus: Philippians 4:13 (NKJV): "I can do all things through Christ who strengthens me." I believe this with all my heart. I am nothing, but He Is All.

Our Lives Were Planned

Psalm 139:13-18 (NIV)

For you created my inmost being;
You knit me together in my mother's womb.
I praise you because I am fearfully and wonderfully made;
Your works are wonderful,
I know that full well.
My frame was not hidden from You
when I was made in the secret place.
When I was woven together in the depths of the earth,
Your eyes saw my unformed body.
All the days ordained for me were written in your book.
before one of them came to be.
How precious to me are your thoughts, O God!
How vast is the sum of them!
Were I to count them, they would outnumber the grains of sand.
When I awake, I am still with You.

This is one of the most beautiful passages in the Bible, for it shows God's unlimited love and pre-destination for all of His created human beings. We aren't what we are today because of an accidental fate. No, no! On God's divine drawing board, He drew out a plan for each and every life. Once, I heard a young woman's account of how her mother always told everyone she was an accident. She was the fifth child and was not planned. The only problem with that statement is that it is a lie.

There are no accidents in God's economy. Is it any wonder that young woman grew up feeling she wasn't wanted, and wasn't worthy of love. It also explained why she was forever seeking man's approval. Her mother didn't know the Bible, nor did her child, unfortunately. For this is the only way we can find our real self and find true unconditional, eternal love.

If one could ever get to know the one true God and His love and plan for His children, they could be healed of every insecurity or poor self-image they carry. Jeremiah 29:11 (NIV) says, "For I know the plans I have for you," declares the Lord, "plans to prosper you and not to harm you, plans to give you a hope and a future."

Yes, bad things do happen to good people. But, when you know the extent of God's love and provision for us, and how He even uses the bad for His good, you know He can be trusted with everything, for He knows best. He never asks anything of us that He doesn't give us the grace to accomplish it. 1 Thessalonians 5:24 (KJV) says, "Faithful is He that calleth you, who also will do it."

If we could ever love the way we are loved, what a wonderful world this would be. He never sees anyone how they are, but only what they can become, transformed by His love.

I heard we are God's masterpiece, put together to be all He has called us to be. I love to do oil paintings, and there is nothing greater than finishing a piece of art that turns out just the way I wanted it to be. What joy, what a sense of accomplishment. Just think, we are all God's masterpieces, made just the way He wanted us to be, what an accomplishment we are to Him. He knit us together to be all He planned for us to be. May we fulfill that call, so we can hear, "Well done, thou good and faithful servant," when He calls us home.

I never have felt that I was truly exceptional is any way. Not in form or beauty, not in my achievements, not in my mechanical or electronic skills to be sure. However, God gave me a wonderful husband who loved me just as I was, and reminded me he thought I was perfect to him. When I was pregnant with my boys, especially with the last one, I was so big. One night, he took the family out to our N.C.O. Club for dinner. I had to go to the bathroom, as pregnant women often do. The ladies room had a full wall mirror that showed everything from about thigh level up. I didn't have anything but a small mirror in military housing. When I got a glimpse at how big I had become, I nearly dropped. Upon returning to our table, I told my husband about the mirror. I told him, "How can you stand to take me out to a public place, I am a wreck." He looked at me and he'll never know how he picked up my spirits that evening. He said, "Honey, I think you look beautiful, I mean it; I have always loved the look of pregnant women." He looked at me through the eyes of love, and I'll never forget it.

That's how our Lord is. He never looks at us any other way. He made us the way we are, and He considers us His masterpiece. If you think you are flawed, just remember, you are a masterpiece in His eyes. Who cares what anyone else sees or thinks? Our world has transformed our view of people by their constantly reminding us of how the world judges our appearance. If you could only remind yourself you are made by Him, for Him and it is the world who has a warped opinion, not you.

Persistent, Personal, Possessive & Perpetual

God's love for us is as written above. It is persistent, personal, possessive, and perpetual. He will not let us share our love for Him with anyone else. He expects our love for Him to be the same. Not only that, but He expects us to have this kind of genuine love for each other.

Real love is endless, eternal, and it doesn't depend upon our performance. Since God is the epitome of real love, why then do we despair when circumstances are such as we either feel unloved by God or His love seems to wane when situations appear to suggest that. What God requires of each of us is a love equal to His great love. He loves us so much that He wants to relate to us personally, persistently, and perpetually, despite what seems to be in our life at the moment.

In the book of Song of Solomon 8:7 (NKJV), Solomon gives a description of real love. He says, "Many waters cannot quench love, neither can the floods drown it. If a man could give for love all the wealth of his house, it would be utterly despised." In other words, no amount of money can buy it. God's love is like that. It absolutely cannot be quenched. It is genuine. When someone or something can kill love, you can be sure that love was never genuine at all. You see, it does not measure up to this description found here in this verse. True love is perpetual. Oh, I am not saying that it cannot be hurt, for I have experienced pain from those I love. I am sure you, too, can relate to that.

No one who has ever been in love with a man, whether it ended in a divorce or not, has not felt the pain of words spoken in anger, or deeds that spurned that love in some measure. Disappointment, doubt, and careless words hurt. But if that love is genuine, it will persist, survive, and continue on. In fact, like God's love, it will forgive, forget, and grow, despite these things. Many a man and woman, despite the pain, were like the Energizer bunny; they kept going and going.

I have met people who were absolutely sure the love they had for their mate once, was damaged, destroyed, beyond repair. Some even ended in divorce. One man who was saved in our church shared with Jim that his wife had left him, divorced, and taken his girls, saying she didn't love him anymore. In fact, that love had turned to hate. He had visitation rights, but he had to pick up the girls at her home. When he would get there, she would send the girls out to the car, so he wouldn't go to the door and she would have to see him. He shared this with his pastor, my husband.

So persistent was his love that our church began to intercede for this family. They prayed God would intervene, repair, and restore this marriage. Everyone realized it would take a miracle of God, but they also knew that with God, nothing was impossible. How did He answer that persistent prayer? Simply believing God, one day, when he was picking up his girls, they didn't run out to the car. It seems his former wife looked out and just couldn't explain why, but she told her girls to let their dad come to the door and knock. He did, pretty confused. His ex-wife opened the door, began talking to him, invited him in, and while she was talking to him, an indescribable love for him overcame her. To make a long story short, he never left the home from that day forth. When he shared his faith with her, how he never stopped loving her and praying for their reconciliation, she also gave her heart to the Lord.

If I was to introduce this family to you today, many years later, you would never believe this could have ever happened to them. Not only did He restore love to them, but did it abundantly and they have had a wonderful marriage since that day. They truly are a testimony to God's restoring and renovating power to a marriage that had been destroyed by Satan and his cunningness. Can He do this again? Yes, but it would be far better if we never let it happen to begin with.

When we make our marriage vows before God, we should mean them and determine in the beginning that nothing will make us break those vows. Yes, I know there are exceptions. If a man abuses his wife, is unfaithful to her, and demands a divorce, nothing but God can change him. If he rejects her love, and demands a divorce, you have God's permission to grant it. Even God makes allowances in this case. But, how many divorces have taken place by people who were in a marriage where they just found it easier to leave than to stay? How many just simply didn't pray and let God work it out? How great is your faith? How genuine is your love? How great is your God?

No one who has been hurt by having a prodigal child forgets the love shown them, and simply rejects the values taught them only to live a life of sin, can really understand the pain they endure. This is as painful as spurned love can be. Yet, many a parent has prayed and received God's grace, which is sufficient. Many still labor in prayer longing for them to be reconciled again. Why? Because nothing, absolutely nothing, can kill that motherly or fatherly love.

All this is said to get us to see just how great a love God has for each of us. In fact, God is love. We can define love by looking at Jesus' love for us. The purpose of that is twofold. Not just to realize how it is possessive, perpetual, persistent, personal, and unconditional, and nothing can kill it. But, we need to know that we must accept and return that love, despite how Satan deceives us into believing God has been unfair to us allowing such difficult circumstances to come into our lives. A few Satan has used on me are my children are not as perfect as others, despite my devoted love and training in God's Word. Yet, I have learned through this how to be compassionate with others who face the same trials, and I probably would have surmised that if others had done such; and such right they'd have had better results.

When my husband, who knew the Word well, would get in the flesh on occasion, I learned God was teaching me that despite his knowledge of the Word, he could get angry also, as others did. I could expect unsaved people to succumb to this temptation from time to time. But I learned that Satan is a worthy opponent, and we are all very vulnerable to his deceit.

I learned words were harmful, and I must choose mine carefully. I learned this by others' words hurting me. Also, since words are so easily misinterpreted, I, as a teacher, had to be extremely careful as I used words in my teaching. I needed to be sure not to say anything that could be misunderstood. I needed to forgive, even if I wasn't wrong. I let God handle the problems, since I would only make them worse if I did it. I learned that God's opinion was far more important than man's. I have had to remind myself that God is in control, not people, no matter how it looks. This has removed much stress.

I am still learning new things. In these last days, I have learned much by being a caretaker. I am learning that pain speaks very loud. Not everything my husband speaks is him speaking, but the pain he deals with every day now, with an extremely bad back. He is short sometimes, he is extremely critical at others, demanding, and is hurtful with words. I have found that this is quite normal when a man is in severe pain. I cannot change the situation, though I pray a lot. But, I can claim 1 John 4:4: "Greater is He that is me, than he that is in the world." And I daily call upon God's grace, which I have found with Paul that it is definitely sufficient.

We have found that the love our family and church family has for us is genuine. Though my two living children live miles away from us, they have come to help us, and believe me they have helped indeed. Our church family has told us to call on them, no matter what we need. They have made it known that they mean that. They have proven those words are true.

What we are going through today is virgin territory for Jim and me. Though these are different types of tests, they are tests to prove our love will be persistent and perpetual. We are finding it has made us more passionate in our love for the Lord. I pray that I will remain faithful as God has, for He is sufficient.

Praise & Thanksgiving

One way I have learned to remember all the areas I want to praise God for, is to list them, remembering a few beginning letters of the alphabet. Like this: I praise the Lord for His:

- ❖ HIS POWER – Unlimited, Almighty. And being my Power Source.
- ❖ HIS PRESENCE – Everywhere I go, He has been there and has promised never to leave or forsake me. Hebrews 13:5
- ❖ HIS PROVISION– All I am or have comes from Him.
- ❖ HIS PROTECTION – Psalm 91 Help me always to remember this.
- ❖ HIS PROBLEM SOLVING – Jeremiah 32:27.There is nothing too hard for Him.
- ❖ HIS PATIENCE – With me and my family.
- ❖ HIS PROMISES – 2 Corinthians 1:20, 5:21. He is a promise-keeper.
- ❖ HIS PRAYER ANSWERS – Jeremiah 33:3. Unlimited amounts.
- ❖ HIS PEACE – In the midst of the storms of life. He makes it a reality in my life, as I trust in Him.
- ❖ HIS PERFECTION – He is perfect in every way. I know that everything in my life is working together for good. Yes, He is good, and yes ultimately for mine. Romans 8:28

- ❖ HIS PERSISTENT LOVE AND FAITHFULNESS–Eternal, unconditional, and doesn't depend upon my performance.
- ❖ HIS PERSONAL, AMAZING GRACE– A gift that is sufficient for all my needs. Grace saved me, secures me, and daily sustains me. Whatever I need His grace is there for me.

- ❖ SALVATION – So costly to you Lord, so free to me. 2 Corinthians 5:21
- ❖ SECURITY OF THE BELIEVER – Titus 3:5-8
- ❖ SECURITY– of our family, our home, our friends, our church, and U.S.A.
- ❖ SPIRITUAL GIFTS – It is your Holy Spirit working through me.
- ❖ SONSHIP – Not religious activity, but a living relationship with YOU Lord. John 1:12, Romans 8:16, Galatians 3:26, 4:6, 1 John 3:1-2.

- ❖ WISDOM AND DISCERNMENT – James 1:5 For living.
- ❖ WONDERFUL WORD – It is alive, and meets my every need.
- ❖ WONDERFUL WORLD – Your marvelous creation, such beauty.
- ❖ WONDERFUL FAMILY– Friends, home, happiness.

YOU are WORTHY! MY GOOD HEALTH, HEALING, RESTFUL SLEEP, UNDESERVED MERCY.

"Giving thanks always for all things unto God and the Father in the name of our Lord Jesus Christ." Ephesians 5:20 (All verses are the KJV.)

Right is Always Right
&
Wrong is Always Wrong

Immorality is always wrong. Purity is always right. There is no middle ground. We would never permit our husbands to have a little affair on the side, would we? Unfaithfulness is disloyalty, and would never be tolerated. It is a breach of trust and contrary to the vows we made on our wedding day. There is no such thing as an open marriage with God, allowing partners the freedom to have as many sexual partners as they wanted. This is always adultery, a sin, and it is always wrong. No matter how many people say different.

Why then do young men and women ignore this part of God's Word and think it is acceptable? It wasn't that they were not raised to know right from wrong. They were taught at home and in church, and some even went to Christian schools. So, we cannot blame our liberal schools. I do believe that those who were home-schooled are less likely to live like this, but it is no guarantee.

To put it simply, this is sin. The consequences are disastrous. Even if a young lady is street smart and has no convictions on abortion, the emotional results are sometimes daunting. Then, there is today the very real danger of contacting Sexually Transmitted Diseases. What a tragedy to have to go through life having to deal with these symptoms such as herpes, not to mention the shame of having to admit you have them. Because God loves us so much, He commanded us not to have sex outside of marriage.

My grandson went to Christian school. One day when in Kindergarten, he came home and told his Mom they had been studying the Ten Commandments. His Mom checking him out said, "Oh, what were they?" When he mentioned, "Thou shalt not commit adultery," she asked him if she explained what adultery was. He said, "Oh yeah, she said it was having sex outside." (What she had said was having sex outside marriage.) We all had a good laugh about this later. But adultery is no laughing matter.

Many lives have been shipwrecked over a "little adultery". Years ago, we knew a young man who shared with us that his sister was having marriage problems. It seems while she was visiting a cousin, she drank too much and was coerced into a sexual encounter. She repented later, but she found out she was pregnant. To cover her discretion from everyone, she had an abortion, telling no one. When she married a fine young man, she was happy and she never told anyone about the abortion. The only thing was though they were married, for years, she never got pregnant. Upon visiting her doctor, he told her she had a botched up abortion and it probably was the reason she wasn't having any success having a child. Her husband and she wanted very much to have a child and the fact they were unsuccessful brought some tension into their home. Though she had confessed her sin to God, and had never told anyone, except her brother, she was torn emotionally, because of her guilt. She was too frightened to tell her husband.

In God's infinite mercy, she was later able to have one child. But the grief and conviction never left her. All because of one little indiscretion. I could share with you many such stories, and the long range emotional damage they brought. There are many physical, as well as emotional scars from sin, but you get the message.

Many men and women simply go on their merry way experimenting with every type of perversion there is. Men gladly participate in such folly. But one day, these people have broken down lives physically and emotionally, and worse, spiritually. Women are no longer attractive and there are always younger, more attractive members of the opposite sex who participate in these orgies.

This is not a pretty picture, is it? Who wants to marry such a used and abused woman? Not many of what we call "good catches". Many a modern-day woman has achieved every success in life and not even thought about a husband or child. But statistics show that there is an innate desire that comes to the surface later, after she has gotten the other out of her system, to be a wife and mother.

I know God still loves men and women who have treaded the roads of immorality. We see in John how Jesus went out of his way to reach one such woman in Samaria. (John 4, any version) He offers them freedom from guilt and shame. But the reality is God loved them before they were even born, and He planned so much better a life for them. You can ignore God's laws, but you cannot ignore the scars.

As I read the Word one day, I thought how well this portrays the U.S.A. today. We have gone astray from what God intended for us as a nation. Even when I was a child, we were called a Christian nation and were proud of it. We knew right from wrong and society backed up what we were learning in school, at church, and at home. It was a wall of protection around all of us. We all had opportunities to choose a different way, but we knew if we strayed, we'd pay too big a price. You see, we would be scorned by our parents, our churches, our neighbors, and society and worst of all, kicked out of school. No one would want to have anything to do with us. Yes, that may seem a bit harsh to many today, but we weighed the consequences and it simply wasn't worth it.

Today, our society elevates every form of deviation on T.V., movies, schools, computers, etc. These appeals elevate the baser level of our fallen natures, and before long, they leave God totally out. This is why many of our pastors are afraid to preach against such sins. They do not want to offend anyone. And after all, they might leave, causing us not to be able to meet our budget. In fact, some of our pastors can't preach certain subjects, because they themselves are guilty of them.

Yes, this is very easy to be used to describe the U.S.A. today. Let's change it. As we see in God's infinite mercy, He is ready anytime we turn from our wicked ways and come back to His ways to forgive us, and heal our land. 2 Chronicles 7:14 (NKJV, emphasis) "If my people, who are called by my name, (Christians) will humble themselves and pray and seek my face and turn from their wicked ways, then, will I hear from heaven and will forgive their sin and heal their land."

Simple ABC's of Prayer

Is prayer difficult? Well, that depends. We must define what prayer is. It is communion (communication) with God. What hinders much of our prayers is time pressure. We simply do not give God our priority in time.

In order to start, we need to **A**cknowledge Who God is. He is our Creator, our Omnipotent, Omniscient, Omnipresent, and All-patient God. He is our Provider, Promise Keeper, Problem Solver, Prayer Answerer, Compassionate, Merciful, Forgiver, Savior, Securer, Sustainer, etc. If you haven't grasped the gist of the first part of prayer, it is Praise and Thanks for Who He Is and What He Does.

Though He wants to communicate with us as friend to friend, He wants us to never forget Who He Is, the Great I Am. Yet, when you have a friend who is in a great position, though you are a friend, you always remember to treat him with respect, no matter how well you know them. You would never take advantage of that friendship asking for special advantages.

When we work hard all day and we pick up dirt along the way, before we sit down on and fellowship with family or friends, we take a **B**ath. We need to do the same spiritually. Out of deep respect, we **C**onfess we have picked up **D**irt (sin), as we have daily walked through this old, filthy world.

We need to approach God with a clean heart. So, confession is definitely a priority.

Since we have now confessed, and are clean, we Expect great things in Faith. How can we limit our God who has placed no limits on our praying? Matthew 21:22, (KJV) says, "All things, whatsoever ye shall ask in prayer, believing, ye shall receive." Now, that doesn't include selfish prayers, or out of God's will. Absolutely, there is nothing too hard for God. Why would we hold back? Especially if we know He is love. 1 John 4:8 says He wouldn't give us anything that wasn't good for us. He will limit us if it is for our good. We must believe He knows what is our best.

Since God has unlimited knowledge, He is worthy to be our Guide. He is omniscient, and since we only know what we see, and what seems right, we must leave our life in His Hands. That is, I trust Him. Remember to pray in Jesus' name. Always remember to pray above all else for the perfect will of God. Sometimes, an answer is yes, but sometimes, God says no. This is no different than we as parents. We would not say yes to a request if we knew in doing so, it would harm them. Never be so stubborn in praying that our will is more important than God's will. I have found true peace only comes when we trust Him completely and accept His will above all else. Believe me; our Lord has just said "No" to me before. I have struggled too, but in the end, I accepted His will for I Knew it was the only way to find true joy. Love compels us to do the right we know to do.

Don't be so worried about praying for so many explicit requests that we miss the fact that He knows our needs even before we pray and knows much more than we do. We can get Mired down in details. And just say "No" to distractions in your prayer life. Satan loves to distract us, disrupt, detour, deter us, deceive, delay us, destroy or depress us. One of the greatest things he does is get our minds off our prayer.

Please put **O**rder in your **P**rayer life. Find a **Q**uiet place:

- Praise and Thank Him.
- Pray for self.
- Pray for your family, immediate and extended.
- Pray for your pastor and your church.
- Pray for Government leaders.
- Pray for others, including missionaries and the persecuted.

Remember to thank God for all His answers. It is the **S**ame as with your children. How would you feel if your children asked passionately for something, and you, out of love, gave it to them? **T**hank Him from your heart, for past, present, and future answers. If your children were **U**ngrateful and never thanked you, you would not feel the same the next time about giving an ungrateful child an answer to their requests? **V**erily, a thank you from the heart makes all the difference to our gracious Lord.

After all this is done, **W**ait on the Lord for His answers. Many problems in our prayer life come from getting ahead of God. His timing is as important as knowing His will. Expect an answer from God, but remember a *no* is an answer too. Not to expect Him to answer is a lack of trust in His prayer promises.

Don't just ask and look for things. Remember, we need to **Y**earn for a relationship with Him as much or more than answers to your requests. He delights to speak with His children. Just like us as parents love to hear from our children, especially if you haven't heard from them in a while. Call on Him; He is waiting for your call.

Be **Z**ealous to do the will of God. That is well pleasing to God. That is what made David such a man after the heart of God. Acts 13:22 (NIV) says, "I have found David, the son of Jesse, a man after My own heart, he will do everything I want him to do."

Don't make prayer difficult. Just simply have a heart to heart talk with Him daily. Bring Him into every area of your life. Like so many of you do with your family and friends, constantly texting each other. I am amazed at how many times people do this. Let's include our heavenly Father and His precious Son in our communication, all day, every day. And we don't even need to type it in. Thinking is a very simple process. If we talked with Him as often as we communicate with others with our iPhones, we would have better lives indeed.

Simple Faith of a Child

Mark, with his parents, was riding to church in their car. In a few minutes, the parents were in a heated argument. Feeling convicted realizing Mark was listening, they tried to tell him it had nothing to do with him, and they were sorry to fight while he was present.

Now, Mark was a deep thinker, and from an early age came out with some pretty profound remarks. But his parents were shocked when he spoke. They had a revival service a few months prior to this and the preacher spoke how Satan's power was limited and we could call on God through prayer and God would bind Satan. Mark simply replied, to his parents "Oh that was really my fault." I don't have to tell you how his parents felt and they immediately said, "Oh, no Mark". He silenced them and said, let me finish. "You don't understand; when we had the revival, I believed what the preacher said, and I prayed that God would bind Satan from our home and not let you and Dad fight anymore. Have you noticed that you all never fight at home anymore, but every time we get in the car, you two begin arguing? I forgot to pray for God to bind Satan from our car, so that you both wouldn't fight in here anymore."

Mark was young, and he had been saved and taught to listen to those who had the authority over him, so he simply believed with his tender heart God was able to do all things through prayer. If only we could grasp these truths with the same faith. Faith opens our spiritual eyes to what God is doing and to what he can do, while others who haven't walked with Him longer cannot understand the activity around them.

Let me tell you about another time Mark showed his spiritual insight. My husband and I often went to Glorietta, New Mexico for training and we stayed with Mark's family, who owned a house there. Jim and I had gone to several troubled churches; Jim having often followed bad leadership. (Like one who had a habit of touching women inappropriately, and another one who stole from the church to the point they were talking about foreclosing on our church. Our church people actually paid off the debt from their own personal accounts.)

My friend in Glorietta suggested we go visit a retired missionary woman who lived there. She was a wonderful lady and my friend knew I would enjoy the visit. Mark, who was a young teenager, went with us. The lady asked me to tell her about my husband and my ministry. I did, and laughing, I told her I sure wish the Lord would put us in an easy church, for once. It would be refreshing. I thought she would share some words of wisdom but to my surprise, Mark said, "Surely, you know why God has placed the two of you in those types of churches, and probably always will." I asked him, "Why Mark?" He said just as simply as if he was telling me it is raining outside, "Why, Jim is a David. He is a warrior preacher. He goes into troubled churches and is used of God to fight the problems. Then, when he solves them, God moves him to another battle zone and sends His Solomon with a quiet spirit to build up His church."

I don't have to tell you we all stood there with our mouths wide open. I knew I had just heard from God through a young man who simply saw through the eyes of faith, what I had missed. I have never forgotten that day. And every time Jim and I got battle weary, we thought of those words.

That was one of our spiritual markers like Henry Blackaby mentioned in his book "Experiencing God".[3]

If a child can simply believe and grasp these truths and take God at His Word, why can't we? There is nothing sweeter than a child's prayer. They have so much trust. And do you ever notice they don't care about anyone else in the room.

Once, when Jim was pastoring in a little country town, I was asked to go to our neighborhood craft time. Most ladies were older than me and I was eager to learn from them. When it came time to eat, I asked if they would like for me to pray. They said they would love it. A little girl, whom her grandmother brought with her, kept asking out loud, over and over, "What are you doing?"

I had just the day before, when the pastor asked us to bow our heads for prayer, seen another little girl. This little girl, probably only three years old, bowed her head, closed her eyes, and grabbed her mother's hand for prayer. God showed me clearly the difference between even children concerning prayer.

Do you want to know more about true prayer, and the simple faith that works? Watch a child that has learned to simply take God at His Word. Luke 18:17 (NKJV) says, "Assuredly, I say to you, whoever does not receive the kingdom of God as a little child will by no means enter it."

---

[3] Blackaby, Henry T. and King, Claude V. "Experiencing God: Knowing and Doing the Will of God". B&H Books; Revised, Expanded ed. edition (September 1, 2008). Originally published June 1976. Nashville, TN.

Simple Hospitality

Who can dispute the part hospitality plays in the lives of Christians? In a world where many are afraid to even speak with their neighbors for fear of WHO they really are, it is more important than ever.

You are probably thinking, "Well, you really don't understand how dangerous it is to invite strangers into your home anymore. You never know if they might be a child molester, or even a killer, a wolf in sheep's clothing." I would be the first to agree, we certainly don't live in the days where keys are left in cars, doors are left unlocked, and kids are running free all over town. Having a son who was an investigator on a large city police dept., I was kept informed about this matter.

Yet, despite the fact we moved around the world, we trusted God to ultimately take care of our three boys. We were mindful of our responsibilities to guard and protect our children. We definitely told them not to be foolish with strangers, even though that wasn't a major problem then.

My husband had prisoners and their families in our home when he was pastoring. We lived in Mexico eleven years after Jim retired. We built a house there where our grandchildren visited. By then, being teens or young adults, they pretty much came and went as they pleased. We had people from church in our homes frequently.

We know bad things still happen to good people. But does that mean we will lock ourselves behind doors and never relate to people, lost needing

Jesus, or saved needing a church family to support them? Lord, let it never be! Where is our trust in God in this? Is He still our Protector, or have we begun doing that ourselves, because He isn't trustworthy?

Please remember NOTHING can happen in the lives of His children that aren't ultimately going to work out for His good. Even if something unexpected happens, it could still happen if we took all the best precautions. You say, but what if something happened? Is God dead? Can He trust you to be strong in His strength? Maybe you are much stronger than you think you are, and He knows you will walk closer to Him through it all. The promise in 1 Corinthians10:13 is that we will not be tested beyond our ability, to get through the trial.

When we were young and moved often in the Air Force, I cannot stress enough how important fellowship was to us. We were rarely near our family and our church family was a necessary support. Open your hearts, and let others in; that includes your neighbors. Do you know their names? Ours don't invade our privacy, but they are near when we need each other.

When I have needed them most, they were there for me. When Jim was in his eighties, and his strength had waned, they shoveled snow for me, offered to cut my grass, some went to the store for me, and some came and sat with Jim so I could go do errands and just encouraged me often. When Jim was dying, they added meals. My church entered into the meeting of needs too. When my son suggested I move closer to him so he could help me, I don't think he understood my telling him I just couldn't leave my church and my friends. Then, when he came to visit during the time Jim was at his worst, and he saw with his own eyes the love shown me, he understood. I am truly blessed, indeed.

I would never feel as safe as I do here. I know how very much I am loved not just by family, but friends and neighbors, as well. I understood that if I moved by my sons, they work, as well as their wives. Friendships take years to build, and I am surrounded by those I love. If God changed my mind, I would leave in a moment. But He hasn't told me yet. Until He does, I am *put*, as my friend says.

Simply a Godly Man

In the simple truth shown by the words of an old friend, I saw what it means to be a simply good person. At the age of eighty-eight, he told us how on an icy road he was rear-ended by another car. When a police officer asked him if he was wearing his seat belt, he didn't have to think over his answer. He simply said NO! He didn't have to think over the consequences of not saying yes, though that would not be the truth. WHY? It was the truth, and he came from a generation that was taught to always tell the truth.

Yet, today so few can separate truth, (reality) from a lie. We live in a world where lying is normal and even accepted. How sad. A mother worries about her little boy going off to an elite college, when he is only four years old. Yet, she neglects the need to teach him the simplest, most urgent character trait, to always tell the truth, no matter what.

It is not enough to simply tell the truth at all times through one's life, but not to do this would be a serious flaw in a person's character. How can we calculate the importance of telling the truth at all times? The most important part of education is molding a child's character.

What if a person excels by the standards of this world, and in the end, he or she cannot tell the truth. Sad to say, lying has become so prevalent, so accepted in our society, that even many Christians think lying is necessary to get ahead in this life. God still says, Proverbs 14:5 (NIV): "An honest witness does not deceive, but a false witness pours out lies." Exodus 20:16 (NKJV) says, "You shall not bear false witness against your neighbor." To be a false witness is to lie. God is the One who promotes. Psalms 75:6-7 (NIV) says, "No one from the east or the west or from the desert can exalt a man. But it is God who judges, He brings one down, He exalts another."

"...See, I have set before you an open door, and no one can shut it;" Revelation 3:8 (NKJV) Today, even men in high places openly tell lies and won't back down when confronted with proof that they lied. This is a terrible way to teach the younger generation, just lie, and never admit it. So many think if they don't lie a little, and work things out, they will never get ahead. All one has to do is watch T.V. and see the times politicians are caught in their lies. They must not know that there is a record of all they say on file. Over and over, they show two different speeches where on each one, the politician takes two different stands on an issue. It is so interesting to see how they will lie their way out of that dilemma.

There's an old song, "A Good Man Is Hard To Find."[4] How true that is. It is rare to find one with this type of character that will simply tell the truth, when doing so might even mean courting harm to him in some way. In the case of this man it meant risking a ticket for not wearing his seat belt though the accident wasn't his fault. I guess police officers have heard every excuse in the book to not get a speeding ticket, but they are used to that, and excuses are just that, excuses. If one breaks the law, he must face the consequences. Anyhow, most officers of the law are more likely to give you a break if you tell the truth.

---

[4] Harris, Marion. "A Good Man is Hard to Find". Composer/Lyricist, Green, Eddie. Label: Victor. February 19, 1919. Camden, NJ.

Simply a Teacher Taught By God

If you ever sat enthralled by a Bible leader teaching a lesson, please remember he or she was simply a person taught by the Lord for the purpose of teaching others. When you ever thank them, always remember Who the Power Source is, God, through His Indwelling Holy Spirit. We, as teachers, cannot do a thing without the Holy Spirit doing it through us. In actuality, we should be thanking God for it is He who is working through us teachers. We are merely microphones. He is using, and perhaps He has spent years teaching that teacher.

As a child, I can thank God for the principles my parents instilled within me. How did I learn them? From watching my parents live those very principles and absorbing them. Truly, they are caught more than taught.

Not only does God teach through those positive things in our lives, but He also teaches us by observing the negatives. Sometimes, I think I learned more from the negatives. My grandmother never accepted me, as I wasn't her blood grandchild, and she verbally mistreated me when we were alone. I learned how to treat all people alike from how she treated me. When my parents found out about what she was doing, they taught me I must still love her for she was older and still was my grandmother. I learned to love the unlovely through this. I didn't understand then, but years later when

Jim became a pastor, that was a valuable lesson. I learned not to retaliate or react, no matter what. I found experience is still a great teacher.

Once Jim started his first pastorate, I found about half the people thought his wife didn't do enough, while half thought she did too much. What a lesson I learned from that. I never would satisfy people, so I'd better find out what God wanted, and do that. If He was pleased, nothing else mattered. I found it would always work, no matter what.

I also learned as a pastor's wife the best thing I could do was to love and care for my husband. I was to make our home a haven of love and peace. Some women work themselves to death at the church at the expense of this haven of rest and their husbands suffer. This doesn't mean neglect your God-given gift or ministry, but it is a matter of priorities. Your husband has many qualified church members, but only one wife. From watching my Mom, I learned what a good wife and mother was. I learned much from her servant spirit. Though, I honestly must confess, I have never measured up to her.

When I was younger, I worked with little children for many years. God gave me a love for them that has never been quenched, even though I teach adult ladies today. I took turns with the Nursery workers during worship services till all my bone surgeries left me unable to work there any longer. You learn so much from these little ones. They are so innocent and honest. They respond eagerly when Jesus calls them. That's how I learned what Jesus meant when He said we must come in childlike faith.

I'll never forget what a child of one of our members said while I was babysitting her. Her grandmother had just died and her parents were busy with funeral preparations. A lady came to my house and said she was so sorry to hear that Linda had died. Immediately, the child of about four or five boldly said, "My grandma's not dead, she's with Jesus." How much faith a child has, it is amazing!

Another child of around eight years old was in Vacation Bible School pre-school, and the teacher was teaching the things that make Jesus happy and the things that make Him sad. At the end of the week, she quizzed them to see what they grasped. "If you are bad all day and disobey your mommy all day what would that do to Jesus? One little girl gave her answer quickly. "He'd get very nervous." Guess where that came from? I'd say that child was being quite honest thinking of her mommy's reactions.

Life experiences are great teachers, but we must couple them with great Bible readings, meditations, chewing them, so to speak, until what we read becomes a part of our being. Deuteronomy 32:46-47 (NIV, emphasis) says, "He said to them, 'Take to heart all the words I have solemnly declared to you this day, so that you may command your children to obey carefully all the words of this law. **They are not just idle words for you, they are your life**. By them, you will live long in the land you are crossing the Jordan to possess."

I can honestly say I cannot separate God's Word from my life. It is my life. So much so that I have told the Lord when He cannot use me anymore, there is no use for me to stick around this old world. Just take me home. I'm ready.

I still love the Word of God. For when I read it, God speaks to me. I often lament those days I studied church doctrine so deeply in Catholic School. What I have often asked myself is what if I'd read and memorized God's Word all those twelve years, that I didn't have a Bible to study? But, God has been faithful to make it up to me by revealing Himself to me. He is so faithful and true. Proverbs 16:25 (NKJV) says, "There is a way that seems right to a man, but its end is the way of death." God's way is the only way.

I believe what James 3:1 (NIV) says, "Not many of you should become teachers, my fellow believers, because you know that we who teach will be judged more strictly." Not many of you should become teachers. Only those called by God, and know it, and are committed to teaching only the truth. For, we will be judged by a higher standard. This is not an excuse for one not to teach, either. It is an admonishment to study ourselves and stay in the Word to be sure of what we teach is true. Not all Bible teachers must have the spiritual gift of teaching. God could use their spiritual gift in the ministry of teaching. But, what is simply needed is for God to call them to teach the Bible. 1 Thessalonians 5:24 (NKJV) says, "He who calls you, is faithful, who also will do it."

Simply, De-Sensitized

Since I am seventy-eight years old, I have seen much in the years past. To me, it is difficult to believe this is the same world as I was living in the 1940's and 1950's. Thus far, I have lived to see my children, my grandchildren, and my great-grandchildren. I have a dear friend who has just recently become a great-great-grandmother. It was a rare event when she went to see that first great-great-grandchild. If I live much longer, I probably will get to see mine, as well. What a world they will be born into.

Unfortunately, we have become de-sensitized by years of progressive deterioration of the morals and culture of our nation. This has happened little by little, as our moral standards have been chipped away. If this had happened overnight, we as a nation would have detected it and immediately did what we could to change it. But as it is, with the slow, subtle changes, each generation hardly noticed how far we have drifted from God's standards found in His Word. Many people have believed for years that they are the final word in all matters of faith and practice. Are they followed as such today?

All we have to do is look around us to see the changes. Hardly a family is not affected. You see, when I was young, church was a vital part of all but a few communities in this nation. It was the center of the community, and few families exempted their lives of worship. Home, schools, government, and the church taught the same morals. There was no disagreement, even if a person didn't have a personal faith in God.

When I went to Cosmetology College, I got the shock of my life. I found several of the young men in our class were homosexuals. Believe it or not, I didn't think there were that many in all our state. I didn't realize how sheltered and naive I was, until then. At that time, cosmetology was one of the professions they hid in. People were sort of expecting an effeminate male in a beauty salon. These young men were likeable, who came to school Monday A.M., showing off pictures of themselves the previous week-end dressed like a woman going "drag" downtown. (Dressed like a woman, looking for a sexual partner.)

Let me get something cleared up right away. They were lost, so they were acting normal. I still learned to love them, but in my heart, I knew this lifestyle was wrong in God's eyes, so also in mine. Why, hadn't God destroyed Sodom and Gomorrah, because of this sin? I tried to witness to them, but they didn't want to hear about God, unless you and He accepted their lifestyle.

Now, we as a nation recently have not only accepted homosexuality as an alternate lifestyle, but we have even recognized marriage between two men or women as a legally accepted lifestyle, giving them the same benefits as a heterosexual married couple. Even after we as a nation of over 200 years said it was a perverted, and a distorted way of life.

Our state, me and my husband are now living in, beautiful Colorado, has also just recently legalized marijuana for recreational use. And as I recall, most of the people fought many times until it finally passed. Talk about change, what is next? I even know some people who say marijuana is less addictive than alcohol, and better for you than smoking a cigarette. Others take marijuana for medicinal use. With all the prescription drugs and herbs on the market, why is that needed? It could damage your influence in this world, and so for that reason alone, we should not use it. We would be presenting wrong for right, and wrong is always wrong, and right is always right. I think it boils down to this, WHO OR WHAT ARE

YOU ENSLAVED TO? Who or what controls you, God or mind-altering substances?

Some say much about those grey areas in the Bible, you know, the ones that are neither black nor white. Something that God has neither said, "Thou shalt, nor thou shalt not." Yet, God has clearly said in 1 Corinthians 6:20 (NIV), 'For you were bought at a price; therefore glorify God in your body and in your spirit, which are God's' and in 1 Corinthians 7:23, we are not to become slaves of men.

Today, many children and young people are confused. You see, schools, government, homes, relatives, the church and yes, their friends, no longer agree in matters of the Bible, homosexuality, morals, marriage, politics, how to raise children, financial management, work ethics, etc. How can we remain a nation undivided, if we have such schisms? One thing is sure, our parents, grandparents, and our forefathers had more successes than we have today. We must return to the basics.

What we need today is not more intelligence, but more wisdom. What we need is not more philosophers, they can't even agree, but what we need is more sanctified common sense. Life is a matter of choices. I have chosen God's Way found in His Bible. Others have chosen the standards of this world. That is their prerogative. That doesn't mean I cannot speak, I cannot choose my own faith, nor read what I choose to read. I have been granted these freedoms under the U.S. Constitution. Our forefathers, guided by Almighty God, foresaw our needs and our Constitution is as applicable today as it was the day it was written. We must choose our own way, and accept the benefits or consequences of those choices. Do we want peace, rest for our souls and the end to all this polarization in our country today? It would do us well to heed what God said to Jeremiah in Jeremiah 6:16-17 (NIV): "…Stand at the crossroads and look; ask for the ancient paths, ask where the good way is, and walk in it, and you will find rest for your souls. But you said, 'We will not walk in it.' I appointed watchmen over you and said, 'Listen to the sound of the trumpet!' But you said, 'We will not listen.'"

God's ways are truly different than satisfying the flesh, but His ways are best. Unfortunately, change is in every area of our country, much polarization, instead of unity. Troubled lives have replaced the serenity of our homes, as well as our streets. Neighborhood relationships have just about ceased in the inner city, as no one trusts his neighbor. Racial riots, and the burning and destruction of businesses are taking the place of loving our brothers as ourselves. Is this a better way than the old ways of our grandparents and our great-grandparents? Their word and a hand shake was as good as a legal paper any day. I personally pray I never will become de-sensitized to this new culture that I believe this is a normal and accepted way of life.

Simply, Forgive Them

Every family, every class, every church, every circle of friends, and every job site has a person who is hard to love. And if it weren't for that one person, we think "how much better life would be."

Though different, they do have some common traits. They stir up strife, are fault finders, accusative, love to pick on people, listen to gossip, drop innuendos, play one person against another, and are back stabbers. If a family was getting together to celebrate, just having that person present, brings a black cloud into the activities.

In an elementary classroom, that person would be a tattle tale, being very careful to appear so innocent themselves. When they get older, they still tell stories, but though there may be some truth to them, they may have embellished them. Sometimes, they are quite hurtful with their gossip. All too often, they are aimed at one person in a group trying to get the group to see how good they themselves are. They often lead in with "I don't mean to sound catty, BUT…."

Women seem to be more prone to these clever, subtle attacks on a person in a group, but it isn't limited to females only. In an office, a person could be male or female, since they both are very ambitious. One way to make themselves look better is to use every opportunity to cut others down. They are eager to get rid of the competition. It doesn't matter who is the present recipient of their vile for two months down the road, it could be someone else they choose.

One of the major similarities of a person like this is they have a spirit of unforgiveness. They cannot forgive nor admit they are in any way responsible for the division they cause. Even if the other person trying to keep peace in the group would accept full responsibility, though not guilty, they would not admit they were a problem. And if they were to say they forgive them, they all too soon demonstrate as they over and over bring up a perceived betrayal. In fact, many years later, you find that they are still dragging up that old dead dog. In a family for instance, no one dare speak up, even though they know the truth for fear of becoming the target. Of course, one way to be assured they won't do that would be to agree with them. That is too high a price to pay. Most times, family members just stay silent. That is good enough.

The only safe way to handle this is to pray, and refuse to let them control your life by making you feel bad all the time. A friend once said when someone accuses you of a certain action or word said, say, "Well I am so sorry you took that wrong. I never meant that and I love you and wouldn't hurt you." If they refuse to forgive and forget, even though you apologize for the offense, just say "Well, I'm sorry you feel that way, but it is your problem that you will have to work out. As for me, I'm sorry for doing anything that would hurt you." After you have done that, it is over. If they bring it up later, could be two years later. Repeat the same sentence. And mean it. Paul said, "Dear friends if our hearts do not condemn us, we have confidence before God." 1 John 3:21 (NIV) Remember, if this person sees you letting it bother you, they will keep it up endlessly.

We once had a man in our church that worried constantly about one member of his family that played these games and kept them disturbed all the time. Every Wednesday at Prayer Meeting, he asked us to pray for his dysfunctional family. One man said, "Oh, Joe, we all have dysfunctional families. We'll pray for them, and you can pray for ours." How true! Here are a few facts we must grasp, in order to understand more clearly:

1.   Satan loves to create dissention. He does his best work when he can keep a family divided, so he works overtime at it. And there is usually a weak person that he can use in any family, church, school, job, etc. So, let's put the blame where it belongs. Satan is the real culprit. Blame Satan, he is the author of whatever the problem.

2.   God allows Satan to work out his evil plot to develop us into a person who can be patient, a reconciler, a pray-er, a mender of broken relationships, an encourager, a forgiver.

3.   We are faced with the choice of having God's mercy and compassion, or giving up on them. What would happen if we did? He or she would be a better tool of Satan, and they just might get more proficient at the game, as time passes.

4.   We need to pray, pray, pray for this person. Not that we can change them, but if we do what God wants us to do, He will change them and in His time.

Once, I had a lady who had been this kind of a divider for years. She even betrayed me and took the word of a lady she hardly knew over mine. "I had it, I said, to myself" "No more, she should be a better friend than that by now." She had known me for years and knew the other lady less than a year. The only problem was all of us in our group loved her husband, who was just the opposite of her, and it would really hurt him. When I was praying about it, the Lord clearly said to me that I had to love her right where she was. She might never change, but she needed me as a friend, and we all had to love her like Jesus loved us. Not where she was, but where she could be and what she could become transformed by God's love. Love and mercy was what she needed, not rejection.

That was years ago. She still remains a friend. Has she changed? Yes, I believe she is far better than she was, but under the right circumstances, she could slip back. But wait, we all could, except for God's grace, mercy, and love.

How many times have we had to go to the Lord for mercy and forgiveness? I believe He is our perfect role model and we must emulate Him and put our feelings aside. There is a verse that means so much to me. Song of Solomon 2:15 (NKJV) says,

"Catch us the foxes,
The little foxes that spoil the vines,
For our vines have tender grapes."

It is the little things that can spoil relationships. If you don't address them, they will grow into major problems. We can't change these kinds of people, but with prayer and us showing them love despite their unlovely ways, they can change. The world is looking for this kind of love. Can it be found in our churches? We are losing our credibility in the world. Could it be because they are looking for a love that cannot be killed by petty problems? They don't know our love is sincere until it passes the test of how it reacts to disloyalty, and a lack of forgiveness.

Simply, It's Only Speculation

A family member hasn't phoned you in over a month. Your mind begins to speculate. Of course, Satan loves this, as it is his opportunity to fill your mind with all types of theories why that person has not called. Since Satan loves to slander God's children, and cause us to stress over the possibilities why this has happened, he begins to work. The tactic that gives us the most grief will be the major one he uses.

One of Satan's best tactics is to tell you, "You must not hurt anyone's feelings, or they won't like you. "Did I say something hurtful, or say something to anger her?" you ask yourself. So, you recall the last time you spoke with her, you know you certainly didn't intentionally say anything wrong. You can't figure it out, yet you worry. You are becoming more stressed with each day. Then, you phone her, as you can't stand it anymore. You are ready to apologize, if need be. But she doesn't answer the phone. Now, you begin to lose sleep over it.

Two days later, you call again. No answer. Now, you are certain you have offended her, and your life is miserable. Then, the phone rings. And who is it? Your sister, all joyful and she tells you she has been on vacation and since returning, everything she'd not done in three weeks has been overwhelming. She is so glad to hear from you and so sorry she didn't call before she left, but with work, and kids, it was so hard getting ready. And suddenly, you realize how foolish you were to speculate.

Now if this worked for Satan, you can be sure it will happen again, though with a little bit of a twist. You go to church and you speak to a friend. She rushes off, and she just didn't act her usual sweet self. That is so out of character to not take time to ask you about your family. And there it goes all over again. Speculation begins. Of course, all the time she had to rush, because her husband was rushing her and they had company coming right after church. But since she didn't know that Satan was up to his old tricks, she repeated the same as last time.

She vows not to let that happen again. But, she finds out her very best friends are speaking hush, hush, when they think she isn't looking. The first thing she thinks is that they are telling secrets behind her back. Maybe she has been left out and she feels she is no longer included. She is hurt, can you imagine she was the one who introduced them. What happened? Why have they excluded her? Speculation begins all over again. Even her husband seems a little quiet lately. Then, you come home one evening. You have been kept late at work. You open your door and all your friends and family jump out and wish you Happy Birthday. What a fool you have been, letting the devil have such a victory in your life. That is what speculation will do for you.

Pastors have to deal with this problem, as well. Jim Smith and family were not in church for two weeks. The first thought that comes to you, are they angry at something I said? Did someone hurt their feelings? Could they be looking for a new church? Of course, he could simply make a phone call to find out the reason, but it is easier to speculate. The same torture is often brought to men who fall into this trap. When he does finally call, he finds out, of course, that it was unnecessary. All is well, except a flu bug has just been through the whole family.

How many times have husbands and wives been trapped by the devil's tactics of speculating whether their mates are fooling around, because of late hours, or being tired, or simply not what they feel the other party should be. It can even happen to a pastor and wife due to unusual hours that have to be kept. What it boils down to, do you trust your mate, or do you speculate at the expense of your marriage? Speculation isn't reality. When I was young, I was told rather crudely, "If you keep your husband happy at home, he won't have to go other places to fill his needs." There is a lot of truth in that statement.

One of the greatest speculations that take place is speculating if a person is lost or saved. This is a curse to the modern day church, as no matter how much we speculate, we cannot know anyone's heart. Only God knows if a person is lost or saved. It is just not our business other than to pray for those we feel need prayer. Yes, Jesus did say that we would know them by the fruit they bear. But, that isn't always true. We know that many things can cause a tree not to bear fruit in one or more seasons, like drought, and disease. But if there is good stock, it can come back and be even more fruitful than before. It is not uncommon for a person to come back to the Lord, after being revived, renewed, and getting rid of sin. Any plant that lays dormant can be revived with the water of God's Word. The fact is one can convince someone they are somebody who they definitely are not. It is all play acting. Some people play the church game well.

How can we go about speculating on a person's spiritual condition? If we do it, we sometimes delay a person's coming back to the Lord from their backslidden condition. Some of Satan's tactics are to distract, deter, delay, detour, distort, and distract us from what God wants us to do. Don't fall prey to his tactics. If we were busy finding God's perfect will for our own lives, we wouldn't be so easy to distract from what God wants us to do right now by the wiles of the devil.

God has given us His Word, which takes out most of the speculation of life. We never have to doubt what He will do. When it comes to the Word, we have a confident hope. If He says it, I believe it, and I can anchor my hope in His Word. Why should I speculate because things look like something else? My hope is not mere speculation. If one does not know all God has promised to do, he cannot take a stand on that promise. But having read God's Word and hidden it my heart, I know I have nothing to fear, not people, and not circumstances, as they seem. He is Truth. He is all I need.

Simply, It's Only Assumption

Another great error we make in addition to speculation is assumption. They are very akin to each other. Speculation is where you make a decision about something, though you haven't seen the event. You theorize or take something to be true, despite not having evidence of the matter. Assumption, on the other hand, is seeing a person or event and without total knowledge of what you see, you determine confidently the truth of a certain event, often wrong.

For example, you see a married neighbor with another woman at the back table of a restaurant, and assume something clandestine or immoral is happening. When, all the while, the neighbor was meeting his sister and wanted not to be disturbed, as they had only a short time to talk.

If the person who saw the above has the tendency to gossip maliciously, this event could well be all over town by the next day, and quite embellished. If she just got on the phone and repeated only what she saw, well if you ever played the game of "gossip," you know what would happen. By the time it was repeated several times, it would be totally distorted.

If the person who saw the event never told a soul, he would've lost respect for the man in the restaurant for no reason at all. The Bible tells us not to let even our good be evil spoken of. "Therefore do not let your good be spoken of as evil." Romans 14:16, (NKJV) But, there are so many innocent events that we never think anyone could twist around. Unfortunately, that isn't always true.

Another good Christian man can stop at a liquor store to get a can of beer for his wife to use in her hush puppies that she is fixing for dinner with fried fish. If he is seen, you can bet the word would be all over town that he was seen buying booze. I can testify that hush puppies made with beer are wonderful. But I would never be so foolish as to go buy even one can. For someone could see me and make a false assumption. So, I just use water or milk and settle for second best.

Now, if this was a fish-fry where non-Christians and Christians would be in attendance, I would make the fact known and get a can of beer from a non-Christian. I'd make known what I was doing, so there could be no assuming I had beer in my home, nor did I drink it.

NOW WAIT A MINUTE YOU SAY! I would like to make a clarification, if I may. I have no problem with those who drink beer and feel it is O.K. I was at that place myself years ago. That was until I talked it over with a visiting pastor. I told him how I felt drinking in moderation didn't hurt me at all, and I thought many Christians were holier than thou. At which time, he explained why he didn't drink any alcoholic beverages, and was convicted not to do so.

First, he said it was a matter of conviction, and he never looked down on anyone who was not yet convicted. He said that was a matter between the individual and the Holy Spirit. He said, like me, the Holy Spirit hadn't convicted me, mostly due to my being a rather new convert. He said he believed he was not an island, and everything he did affected those around him. He went on to explain that many take one drink, and because of their compulsive nature, cannot stop at one. If I offered them a drink, and they drank it, they might leave my home, over-indulge somewhere else, have an accident on the way home, and end up killing a child. I would have been complicit in that child's death, despite being ignorant of his problem. My giving one drink, or by my testimony that it was O.K., could set into motion all types of destructive ends.

Actually, I had never been presented with this scenario before, but I had seen the destruction of lives due to alcohol in the past, and I could agree with him. After that talk, I WAS CONVICTED! That very moment, I could never look at drinking the way I had all my life. I realized God wanted to use my life, and I didn't want anything to detour that. That day, I made a vow to the Lord to never let alcohol tough my lips again. Nor would I ever give anyone cause to speak evil of my good.

If you are not convicted equally, I never look down on you. I am not the Holy Spirit who brings conviction, so who am I to tell anyone else what or what not to do. I am aware of all the times in the Bible that wine was used, including Cana. And I know all about the types of wine served, etc. That has nothing to do with your decision, or my decision. God is a big God. He is able to tell you what He wants you to do. I just can share why I believe the way I do. It was many years later that Jim was called into full-time pastoring. God saw this, and He prepared my life and Jim's a long time before that.

People hold some pastors in such high regard that they think they should not even give a hint of wrongdoing. They assume they are perfect. Unfortunately, they have such high expectations of them that they make many false assumptions about them. They even think they are judgmental when they preach the Word of God. It isn't the pastor, but the Lord who is judging their life. People even judge retired pastors. Some are getting quite old and no longer preach, teach a Sunday school class, go out on scheduled visitation times, etc. So, people assume they are not doing what they asked others to do. Do not assume they are not affecting the lives of others by contributing to the lives of others wherever they go. Any wisdom they have just oozes from their life and words. God still uses them.

One of the times people assume things they shouldn't is in the death of a loved one. Do not assume because of one's vocation, like a police officer, that someone in authority must remove all guns, or due to severe pain they will commit suicide. This is a false assumption. This happened when my son was dying, and it brought great anxiety to him. He was a sold-out Christian and never even thought of suicide as a possibility. I know some have done so, but people should have known better of him.

A great false assumption is that if a loved one does not cry and show open grief at a funeral, the person surely didn't love the dead person. People handle grief differently. And the very fact portrays just the opposite. The Bible clearly says we are not to grieve the way the world does. 1 Thessalonians 4:13, (NKJV) says, "But I do not want you to be ignorant brethren, concerning those who have fallen asleep, lest you sorrow as others who have no hope." If there is joy, it is because of the person's walk with the Lord. They are convinced that person is with the Lord, and has entered his or her rest, and is free of all the sorrows and sufferings of this old world."

Our faith walk does affect our emotions. Grace allows one to carry on during the ultimate release of a person to new life. It is not a lack of grief for a loved one. We do have promises we will see our loved one again. However, when we see God and His Son, our loved ones will follow. Not that these relationships will be the same.

Rather than assume the worst of people, let us make some positive assumptions we can honestly make due to the Word. Do assume God will meet yours, as well as everyone's, every need. I cling to Isaiah 54:5a (NIV), which says, "For your Maker is your husband-the Lord Almighty is His name…" Now that my husband has died, God is my husband. It doesn't matter that my family is scattered all over the U.S.A. God loves, God cares, God sees, and God hears. He is also in control of my life.

Do assume you will never end up in financial depravity, destitution. If God created you and the world, and owns the cattle on a thousand hills, can He not provide for those left behind, yes, even you too?

Do assume God protects all His children for He has told us not to fear anything, just God alone. 1 John 4:18a, (NKJV) says, "There is no fear in love; but perfect love casts out fear, because fear involves torment…" So, we have no need to fear being alone, or living in a crime zone. Assume God is your protector. Read Psalm 91.

Do assume God has the final say in all matters. God works mighty things out at funerals, and later, as the result of something said that day. Every pastor needs to tell the loved ones that the person in the casket will never see a loved one again, unless they have experienced salvation through the imputed righteousness worked out at Calvary. Jesus was our substitute, and we are only accepted by what He has done. 2 Corinthians 5:21, (NIV) says, "God made Him who had no sin to be sin for us, so that in Him we might become the righteousness of 'God." Romans 6:23, (NKJV) says, "For the wages of sin is death, but the gift of God is eternal life in Christ Jesus our Lord."

Simply Put, The Old & New Covenant

One of the hardest things for a Christian to understand is the way the Bible is divided. It really took me many years before I understood the connection. So, I will strive to explain it as simple I can. If you are a new Christian, or one who just hasn't quite got the message, I hope this helps. Remember, I will not try to do a Bible Study out of this, just make the connection, so you can better understand.

Getting down to basics, the Bible is made up of two major divisions, the Old Testament and the New Testament. Let's first define testament, so as to better understand. Simply put, testament could best be understood as a contract, a pledge, or a covenant made between parties. Most of us are familiar with these things. The Old Testament was a contract between God and man. Like our modern contracts, it is a binding agreement. If one party reneges, it is void. It is normally written and legal. Although we know, in my grandfather's day, many men made verbal contracts and sealed them with handshakes, I doubt in our society, we could trust any man or woman to do that.

In our days, there are many forms of contracts. We sign a marriage contract when we pledge to love and remain faithful to our mate. We pledge to pay Sears, or some other company, so much on our credit card, so we can buy a new washer, dryer, or other appliance, until it is paid in full. We sign a contract pledging to pay a house payment over a twenty or thirty year term. This allows us to live in said house, while our bank really owns it until it is paid for, and then we get the deed. Countries also sign pacts with other countries, where a larger more powerful country promises all their resources will be available to the other country, if they allow us to have, for example, a military base on their land. Both parties are responsible to keep the terms.

The Old Testament was a covenant, or contract, of Law. God made promises to Israel, His people. In return, He made demands of them. If they obeyed these terms, obeyed His laws, they would receive promised blessings from God. Also, God demanded blood sacrifices as part of the terms. He told them exactly how He expected them to offer these, and demanded obedience to all His laws. The benefits Israel would receive hinged upon their pledge of obedience. Most of these terms were merely symbolic, pointing to, or a portrayal of, the coming New Testament. Later, they would clarify the New Testament, which would replace the Law with Grace.

When Jesus came and died on the cross at Calvary, the terms of the Old Testament were fulfilled and the New Testament replaced the former. This covenant was better than the Old Testament, because it was a testament of Grace, (Gift) not of Law. Jesus paid the debt of sin once and for all at Calvary. He became our substitute, and died for the sins of all who would accept that free gift. Ephesians 2:8-9, (KJV); Hebrews 7:27-28, 8:6 (KJV); John 3:16 (KJV); 2 Corinthians 5:21. (*Imputed*) righteousness is a bookkeeping term and it means our account is forever paid in full. We no longer need to keep the Law for salvation, but because we are saved. Grace has replaced the Law. We now have entered into a living, intimate relationship with God, through Jesus Christ, and are declared sons of God. Galatians 5:26-29, (KJV). We have become completely immersed in Christ and are heirs, by what Jesus did for us at Calvary. It is a gift, it is grace. We cannot earn it, buy it, and certainly don't deserve it. Romans 4:4-5 (KJV) 2 Corinthians 5:21 (KJV) This is not a free license to sin, but if we do sin, He forgives us because of what Jesus did.

While Jesus was on this earth, He was authenticated by the miracles He performed. When He left, He left His Holy Spirit and His Apostles were authenticated by these, as well. Our salvation is authenticated by our changed lives. The Holy Spirit living in us is the power that changes us. Only God can take a man like Paul from being a persecutor, to be persecuted for the same faith he put others to death for.

God didn't abandon Israel when the Gentiles believed in Him and the age of grace came into place. God simply let a temporary spiritual blindness come upon Israel until the last Gentile (non-Jew) that is to be saved will be. Then, when the Christians are all gone, the blindness will be removed and they will realize Jesus was truly the long prophesied Messiah. This is what is spoken of in Romans 11:25-27, (KJV). Once again, Israel will get the status as the children of God, and they will all be saved. The Jews will once again be chosen by God to become the 144,000 evangelists, but only during the Great Tribulation. This is when the Jews will be used of God to witness to the present lost world. As Daniel wrote about, the last seven years that has been allotted to the Jews will take place during the Tribulation. The Age of Grace will have ended and the church will be gone. The Holy Spirit, as the Indweller, will be gone. He is our Power Source today. So, the task given to the Jews will not be easy.

I pray this helps you to better understand these two ages. We should never turn our backs on Jesus' grace, it truly is amazing, and was very costly to God and His Son. I shared how I was a Catholic before I was saved. One of the greatest woes was not to know for sure where I would go if I died during the night. What a comfort to know it is all of grace, not of works. I am so glad I have lived during the Age of Grace. It is all of relationship, not religious activity. Jesus paid it all, all to Him I owe, as the hymn says.

Simply Put, What the Bible is to Me

There is only one verse that says what the Bible means to me. Deuteronomy 32:47a, (NIV, emphasis), which says, "They are not just idle words for you, (Terri) they are your life."

Nothing else can describe the importance of the Bible to me. I am so passionate about its importance to that every time I read it, or teach it, the words of Jeremiah best describe how it burns within me. I have an inborn drive and cannot hold it back. It is truly like a fire burning. I must let it out. Jeremiah 20:9, (NIV) says, "But if I say, I will not mention him or speak any more in His name, His word is in my heart like a fire, a fire shut up in my bones, I am weary of holding it in, indeed I cannot." It is a burning passion to me.

For years, I never had the Bible, which I believe is the written Word of God, in my hands. But, like Jeremiah 15:16, (NIV) says, "When your words came, I ate them, they were my joy and my heart's delight, for I bear Your name O Lord God Almighty." They became a part of my very being. You cannot separate them, for they are me. You have heard the saying "we are what we eat." How well that describes me spiritually. I feed on them and they are me.

Once a man told me I talked about the Lord and His church too much. "Didn't I have anything else in life to talk about?" Without thinking, I told him, "Well, I guess the reason I talk so much about them is they are my life." After I thought about that a bit, I realized just how true those words were, and they really didn't come from me. That doesn't make me pious, or better than anyone else. I am simply a sinner, saved by grace. But that doesn't keep me from lifting up the ideal though I have, and still, do miss the mark. Despite my failures, the knowledge I have learned experientially, has taught me that the closer I follow His Way, the better my life is.

Actually, we are daily being conformed to the world or being transformed by the renewing of our minds. Romans 12:2, (NKJV) says, "And do not be conformed to this world, but be transformed by the renewing of your mind, that you may prove what is that good and acceptable and perfect will of God." Whether we realize it or not, our minds are being saturated by modern day media and I believe we must stand against that. Instead, we must saturate our minds with the things of God. Not just read the Word, but meditate upon it, eat it, and chew it, until it becomes a part of our being.

The very tools I use to make my teaching easier, especially my computer and printer, can be used for the very opposite, to corrupt my mind. Although I have struggled to become computer savvy, I often wonder what I would do without it. Yet, others I know are using modern day technology to corrupt their minds and souls, especially young people. Not to mention how the devil has used them on our modern day pastors. My husband was appalled how so many computers keep pastors glued to them, at the expense of their being out evangelizing the community. We have heard every excuse there is why not to get out of the church building and go where the people are to witness to them. This technology is often a modern day curse, depending on Who or what controls you.

I cannot aptly describe what happens to me when I hear a man mishandle the Word of God. If a man plays in the pulpit, I want to jump up and yell, "You're wasting precious time, get to the Word." People haven't come to hear loquacious jokes, or your twenty minutes of eloquent introductions to introduce you to a ten minute Biblical sermon. I often find there are more public speakers than preachers in our pulpits. Usually you hear more entertainment than a message on atonement in our churches today.

The Word is powerful. It is not a pastor's words that change lives. If our pastors will just be faithful to proclaim God's Word, lives would be changed from hearing it, not him. What a waste! God has so much to say to us, no matter where we are with the Lord. I often sit and wonder why the preacher is not quoting more of what God says about the topic that is being preached. I'm really not interested in his trying to convince me of scientific or philosophic ideas. And for goodness sakes, don't try to be a man-pleaser, withholding sensitive controversial topics. It is so obvious to the spiritual man.

If a man spends much time alone with God, it will sure make a better preacher out of him. It will overflow into his life, become his life. He won't be able to hold it in. He will simply become a microphone that God uses to speak to men and women. Jesus is the Living Word and He speaks to us through His Written Word. You just cannot separate the two.

Yes, the Word of God is a treasure. If you have had this treasure collecting dust, get it out and read it. Let it become your life too. It is so exciting and you will be fully equipped to be used of God. 2 Timothy 3:16-17, (NKJV) says, "All Scripture is given by inspiration if God and is profitable for doctrine, for reproof, for correction, for instruction in righteousness, that the man of God may be complete, thoroughly equipped for every good work."

Simply Put, Zip Your Lips!

James 3:1-12 says so much about the tongue. Even though the tongue is a small member of the body, it can be deadly. In fact, James says that one way we prove we are mature in the Lord is if we can control our tongues. Not how many times we go to church, not how many classes we teach or how many committees we serve on, or how pious we are, but by the way we use our tongues, or our speech.

We know how much can be done with our speech, it is what a man uses in the pulpit to preach the Gospel, and many are turned from sin from that sermon given by God. But we also know how it can be used to damage the cause of Christ. The fact is we use it for both good and bad, at times. The results can be destructive, or for God. The former should never be so. How can we gain control over this terrible dilemma?

For one thing, the same member of our anatomy will surprise us sometimes. It takes much prayer if you are a very verbal person. I'm afraid I have sometimes spoken too quickly, or didn't think before I spoke. It isn't always what you say that gets you in trouble, it's how your words are taken by the person being spoken to. So, we have to not only make sure we don't say the wrong thing, but think about how our words may be taken.

My granddaughter was chatting away one day while my son and I were listening. He says to me, "I swear that child has never had a thought pass through her head that didn't come out of her mouth." I laughed, but then I really thought about that, and decided that happens to a lot of adults too. I think I was so much like her when I was a little girl. If they ever needed anyone to speak in school, they'd call on me, for I always had the words and never feared talking in front of people. Thank God, she and I have matured enough to know that I must really think about what I say when I speak. That is even when I teach a Ladies S.S. Class. I have to be so careful that it is God speaking and that He is my Power Source. My words could sure get me in trouble. Not that I would back down, because the words from the Bible are very convicting, but I must not add to God's words.

Even when God speaks to us, it doesn't mean we are to repeat it to those who aren't ready to hear it. In Genesis 37, Joseph learned that. He was such a good example as what we share can get us in a lot of trouble. Remember how he shared his dreams with his brothers. He was young, and didn't think this revelation through. They weren't very spiritual and little did Joseph know that the result would be their thinking he was boasting, and they became jealous, resentful, bitter, and vengeful toward him. His father didn't even understand what his words meant, but at least he was spiritual enough to keep the matter in his heart.

Of course, God, being omniscient, knew the havoc Joseph would wreak and He worked right in the middle of the situation. He always does, for His good. "And we know that all things work together for good to those who love God, to those who are the called according to His purpose." Romans 8:28, (NKJV) But, it sure would've been easier if God had worked it out without having to pick up the broken pieces we strew along the way.

God used the matter to get Joseph to Egypt, and despite all the problems along the way, He put Him in a high position where God could use him to save His people from famine and the whole family's life, as well. It is obvious God used this situation to not only grow Joseph into the man he became, but his brothers' lives as well.

How much hurt has been caused by a spoken word without pondering and praying beforehand? The examples of the spark turning into a forest fire and the small rudder guiding a huge boat, and the need to control such a small, though poisonous, member of our body, are so awesome. It took me years to bring my tongue under control and I still have to work at it, as I am a very verbal person. We cannot use that as an excuse.

Yes, sometimes we just have to zip up our lips, and even bite our tongues till we draw blood if needed, rather than say something we will be sorry for.

Simply Put,
Temptations Appeal to Us

Let's get honest about this subject. Satan is very real, and he is very clever. Though not like God, all-knowing in all matters, he knows all our vulnerable areas to attack. This comes from his studying all of us and searching out our areas of weakness. But, he cannot make us do anything, despite what Bill Cosby says, "The devil made me do it," he cannot make us do anything.

We see starting in Genesis, the first man and woman and how the serpent started it all, "the Blame Game," that is. The man, Adam, blamed the woman, and the woman, Eve, blamed the serpent. This is one sport we like even more than baseball or football, *pass the buck* it is called. And have we learned to play it well.

Temptations come in different forms and are many and very diverse, depending upon the weakness of the person being attacked. With our liberal society, we are being bombarded with a media that portrays all forms of degradation that are directly against God's will for His people and many lies to tell you how right it is. Is it any wonder why many Christians are succumbing to temptations?

Some of our greatest most useful inventions like the Internet, computers, tablets, and smart phones with search engines like Google can bring in the bad, as well as the good. They will answer any question you need an answer for, but at the same time, tell you where you can find any type of pornography that might appeal to you. And they change so quickly, trying to keep up with it is extremely frustrating, especially to parents who aren't really tech savvy. I'm so glad my children and grandchildren are keeping up with this, and not me.

How great it was to live in the time I did. We were so protected from the world in the 40's and 50's. Can you believe I never saw at T.V. until I was a teenager? Not only that, but there was only a few shows on T.V. and they had to be clean or they didn't meet the standards to be on the air. Every Saturday, we as kids went to the movies. My parents didn't have to worry about what was playing, because it was for kids and it was always clean.

We ran free all over town, the biggest worry our families had was if we were going to pay attention to the time and be home for family meals. No one worried about having obese children then, there was very little junk food on the market and we only had candy at Easter and Christmas. Not to mention there was no such thing as *bussing* under a mile from school.

Some of us old fogies were reminiscing not long ago about our school years. What laughs! We remembered when we got our mouths washed out with soap if we dare say the S--- word. If the school teacher disciplined us, we didn't dare tell our folks, we would get another spanking at home. Our parents told the teachers to discipline us if we needed it. There was no danger of suing back then. Many evenings we remembered having to write, "I will not talk in class" 100 times. I would get so angry I wanted to scream, but there was only one way to get out of it. Don't Do It! What a change in our schools today. Discipline? What is that?

Probably the greatest problem I have seen in my days is in pastors and their wives. I can say this for I was one, my husband was a pastor, and what is happening today was unheard in the days he was pastor. Satan seems to be attacking them in a way we have never seen before. One pastor's wife confessed to her prayer partners that her husband was addicted to pornography. Another we heard of was caught in an adulterous relationship. And in the city newspaper in one of our large cities all over the front pages was the report that a male lover of one of the pastors of a large church was in a homosexual relationship with him, and had been for quite a while. And despite this fact, he preached against this sin of homosexuality in his church.

So many of the tasks we assumed belonged to the pastor in days gone by are not thought to be their responsibility anymore. If they prepare and preach a sermon, this should be all that is demanded of them. The rest should be done by others. Not that there isn't some truth in that, but they should lead out and men will follow. So many pastors' wives believe they have no accountability to anyone. It's their husband's call, not theirs. Whose will is all this, the Lord's, or their own agenda? Perhaps, they wouldn't have time to get into these ungodly situations if they devoted themselves to the work of the Lord.

Many people have given themselves over to the devil. They don't even fight against the tempter, for if they did, they would not live like they do. James 1:14-16, (NKJV) says, "But, each one is tempted when he is drawn away by his own desires, and enticed. Then, when desire has conceived, it gives birth to sin, and sin when it is full-grown, brings forth death. Do not be deceived my beloved brethren." Hebrews 2:18, (NKJV) says, "For in that He Himself has suffered, being tempted, He is able to aid those who are tempted."

They have all the power to overcome these temptations, but they do not any longer ask for help. They love their sin, and if not physical death, it will end up with the death of their ministry. Malachi 1:6-8, in his day prophesied against the priests who God had said despised His name. They wanted to know how they had despised God's name. They had permitted Israel to offer blemished sacrifices ignoring the Law. Also they had taken idol worshipping women for their brides, and the priests didn't condemn them. Today, pastors simply do not preach the whole counsel of God for the people do not want to hear it. Many of the fleshly sins, they themselves are committing.

1 Corinthians 10:13, (NKJV) says, "No temptation has overtaken you except such as is common to man, but God is faithful who will not allow you to be tempted beyond what you are able, but with the temptation will also make the way of escape, that you may be able to bear it." Only one thing is necessary, CALL FOR HELP! That is, if you really want help?

Simply put, we sin today because it appeals to our fallen nature. We have the Holy Spirit in us to empower us, but we love sin so much, we just ignore all the resources available to us. The only reason we don't have victory over sin is because we really love it so much; we make it a practice, not thinking about the consequences to us and God's church. If I yield control to the old nature, I'll fail. If I yield control to God, He controls and overcomes temptation through me.

Our churches are rapidly losing their credibility in the world today. People are fed up with pastors and they are fed up with compromising Christians who play the church game. These people are hypocrites which the world sees, despite how the try to cloak it. They hold up a mask and pretend they are a committed Christian, while their lives tell a different story.

We can have a restored relationship with the Lord; it is just a breath away. It is called confession. 1 John 1:9, (NKJV, emphasis) says, "If we confess our sins, He is faithful and just to forgive us our sins and to cleanse us from ALL unrighteousness." I am not one of the few who say it is too late to change, we have gone too far. I realize we are very close to getting there, but each time people have turned around, God has forgiven, forgotten, and He is ready to restore again.

Simply, Subtle Temptations

Satan has so many tactics, and not all are easy to detect, as they are so subtle. I have dealt with him on many occasions, and have had to go to the Lord for help. The Lord has pointed out to me one way to recognize how He operates is to think of words that begin with the letter "D". Let's begin, and I hope this might help you also, as you try to detect him.

God makes clear what my first priority in service is. I am to teach women. Since I love this task and am very committed to plan, prepare and be ready each Sunday to teach my Sunday school class, Satan will Distract me regularly. You know, I'll get some urgency in my immediate family, something I cannot help but be concerned about. It doesn't necessarily need my doing anything, but I am concerned about it, and it dominates my mind. Satan knows my commitment will be met, but I will not be able to give my teaching my 100% concentration. After all these years, it still makes it so hard to keep my attention on what I am called to do.

Distractions come in many forms, and are usually good things which can easily distract. Your family can be Satan's #1 tool of distraction. I have seen it in my own life and I see it today in others' lives. Since my mind tends to wander, Satan loves to cause me to think of a million things when I should not let them distract from what I am doing. An example is when I am praying. But, I have to admit I am guilty of this many times. It is one thing to know theoretically this is what is happening, and another to overcome it through calling on God's help.

Another tactic used by Satan is Disruptions. Have you ever noticed how many times your quiet time or your study time has been disrupted? Maybe it was a phone call, maybe a doorbell; maybe your husband, a child, or a neighbor needed you. I have even been interrupted by my husband to tell me of some news flash that he thought I need to hear. But, when you get back to your studying, you just can't pick up where left off. Your whole train of thought has been interrupted. Since my children, grand-children, and even great-grandchildren are not near me anymore and live from one coast to the other, I can't blame them. But I have noted if I really don't want to have my time alone with God disrupted, I have to get up early, and take the phone off the hook, which I have a hard time doing. I always feel I might have an important call.

If Satan can just Detour, Deter, or Distract me from that which I need to do now, he has accomplished that which he desires to do in my life. I have a wonderful ladies Sunday school class, and if they can be there each Sunday they are. But, I want to visit with them more, get to better know their innermost needs. You just cannot imagine the tactics Satan used to detour and deter me from doing what I know to do. I don't know what I'd do if it wasn't for the good old telephone. I want to be able to take a pot of soup whenever a neighbor or lady in my class is sick. Isn't it coincidental that these are the very times when I have many demands on me already? NOT!!!

If Satan can just get me to put off for tomorrow, that which I should do today, he is so pleased. Who knows what tomorrow brings? This is another tactic of the devil, Delay. He never tells us not to do some good deed. He simply has us put it off one day at a time. Then tomorrow, he will come up with a new reason for us to put it off again and again. Oh my! I am not as much a procrastinator as I used to be, but it is one of the character flaws that I and others with my same personality have. Since

Satan studies me so he can find my weaknesses, he can sure know what I myself know about me. He is aware of all my flaws, and he uses them against me.

Often, God lets us boast about all the things we will do tomorrow or sometime in the future. Yet, He knows we do not know what tomorrow holds. My father-in-law always talked of the things he would do when he retired. He lived on the water, had a boat, and all the fishing equipment needed for the retirement life, yet he never did get to do any of it. My son died at age 54. I'm sure he dreamed of all those things he would get to do when he finally retired for good. But it never happened. James 4:13-14, (KJV) is good advice for us. If there is any good we need to do, now is the time for us to do it. We may not have a tomorrow.

Sometimes, Satan gets us to only put off for an hour some special thing God wants us to do. How many times has he succeeded at getting you to even do a household chore, by side-tracking you with the thought, 'Oh, I'll just do it in an hour or so.' The problem is that hour passes and you simply don't get around to it, because something else comes up.

My general health is very good. But, I am ever reminded of how quickly God could take me home if He so willed. In the past year, we have lost three of our closest friends to death. My husband's two best friends died. I have lost one of my good friends in that year. If you had told any of us a year and a half ago that now three of us would be gone, it would almost be unbelievable. The oldest of the six of us is still alive, and the others are at home with the Lord. I believe they are the fortunate ones. We did many wonderful things together. We even spent eleven years in Old Mexico serving the Lord by doing volunteer missions. We went out to dinner and played cards every Friday evening for nearly twenty-seven years. That part of our life is gone. Jim and I believe we are here, because God is not finished with us yet.

If anyone believes in the inerrancy of the Bible, it is me. No one could believe more than I do that it is true from the first page of Genesis to the maps, as one man said. Yet, I am not immune to times Satan tries to trip me up with Doubt. God's nature is clearly shown over and over in His Word. Like in the Garden of Eden, Eve was Deceived by Satan who simply said, "Did God really say…? (or mean?) Or, is He really a God of absolute love when He allows such and such in someone's life? Can He be responsible for such a great creation? (All of it, after all, must be proven). Could God ever stand by and let young girls get kidnapped and raped? Just how does that fit in with a God of power and love?

I have had to wrestle with some thoughts implanted in my mind like these. But, thanks be to God, He doesn't hate honest questions from His children. The determining factor is, did we get through those times, and come through them stronger than we were before? For me, I received answers to my questions. God said to me, "Do you trust Me in this?" "Am I not powerful enough to get you through this?" "Is My love, power, grace, love, and control not sufficient to sustain one through this?" "Remember, I am unlimited in knowledge, power, grace, patience, presence, and love." "I see, I care, I know, I will act and settle all." What a lesson this is. Doubts truly are stepping stones to a higher level of faith. What matters is what we do when these Doubts come.

One of Satan's tactics which affects so many people today is Debilitating Depression. It is a mega-destructive force or attack from Satan to stop his arch-enemy God, and His work. Webster's Dictionary defines it as a psychoneurotic or psychotic disorder, marked by among other things sadness, feelings of dejection, hopelessness, reduction of activity, and sometimes suicidal tendencies.

To put it simply, it can be so disabling and devastating that a person is emotionally paralyzed. One is stopped dead in one's tracks. He or she cannot even think straight. One is so consumed by one's problems that his or her life has just about ceased. What one needs is not medications or prescriptions, legal or illegal. (Many today in Colorado, who have never even thought about using marijuana, have been convinced it can help them with all sorts of ailments, since it has been legalized.) What is really needed is deliverance and that only comes when one commits all he or she is to the Lord and lets Him save and deliver him or her. Even a true Christian can yield one's life to these things we've mentioned. If for one moment we are deceived by Satan and trust in anyone or anything other than the only Savior and Deliverer Jesus Christ, we can fall into Satan's trap.

We must realize this is serious business and if you yield one inch to the devil, he will not stop until he fully controls you. Our pastor just put up a sign in front of the church that says, "If you give Satan an inch, he'll become your ruler." So true! I know there are such things as hormonal and chemical imbalances, but those can be treated physically. This is not what I am writing about. The devil has come to Destroy; that is his intention and these are some of his tactics. (1 Peter 5:8, 2 Corinthians 2:11, Ephesians 6:11, I John 3:7-8)

Remember to take note of the D's when you ponder Satan's tactics. BEWARE, he is a worthy opponent. (Ephesians 6:10-12) Call for God's unlimited power when these terrible D's pop up in your life. They are very toxic. "Submit to God, resist the devil and he will flee from you." (James 4:7, NKJV) "Therefore submit to God. Resist the devil and he will flee from you." (1 John 4:4, NIV) "You, dear children, are from God and have overcome them, because the one who is in you is greater than the one who is in the world." Claim these verses.

Simply, Supernatural: Part I

Nothing could adequately explain my husband's and my life except with the word supernatural. There is nothing magical about it. It is simply beyond natural explanation. It has been and is all of God. God has simply taken two very unimportant people that were hardly capable of doing much due to their lack in talents and education, and done impossible things through them.

What an adventure it has been to see the hand of God moving in putting us in so many different places for His service. I have heard Jim say on many occasions that God sent him to use him for the Lord, and used the Air Force to pay our way and get us there.

While Jim was in the Air Force, you could swap orders if you were the same rank and career field. How does a man come up to you and say he'd like to exchange orders with you to go on an isolated tour to Taiwan and let you have his orders for you to go to Germany with your family? It just doesn't happen, but it did. The isolated tour was just one year long and the Germany tour was for three years. The other guy had been to Germany and he didn't want to go back.

Another time someone exchanged orders with Jim, and he got a "cushy" basic electronics instructor's assignment in Biloxi, Mississippi. This G.I. didn't want to be an instructor, so he exchanged orders. Jim had to go up a mountain at a radar site in Southern California. Jim had already been to Biloxi for a year's electronic school, and we really liked the church there.

Wherever we went, we were able to go together, and wherever Uncle Sam sent, there was a church home waiting for us. We grew immensely in those years. When we went to Germany, we were stationed with the Army where Jim was a Forward Air Controller. He had a jeep with lots of electronic equipment, and they went ahead and called the airplanes in on target. They had trained him to do this in Vietnam; however, God never allowed him to be sent there.

While in Germany, we started a church, as there was none there, with the help of the Hanau Baptist Church. A German Lutheran church also helped us and we met before their services each Sunday. They were happy to do it, as they said the Americans had helped them greatly after the war. While there, Jim took our R.A.'s to a youth hotel on the Rhine River for a retreat. While he attended a counselor's meeting, like normal boys will do, they had a big pillow fight. These were feather pillows, also there was mold, and lots of dust. When Jim came back he had a terrific asthma attack, as he was allergic to all of the above. All were stirred up from the fight. He ended up at the USAF hospital in Frankfurt, Germany, as he could not overcome the asthma attack. They air-evacuated him to the States. They sent him in the States to San Antonio, Texas, where he was in a lung ward. This left me and our three sons in a foreign country all alone without Jim who had always done all the business of moving from one location to another.

This all happened so quickly that my head was spinning; I didn't know where to begin. Since we had been instrumental in beginning the work in Aschaffenburg and it was doing well, I couldn't understand why the Lord was allowing this to happen to us. Then, I got a call from Jim's Commanding Officer who told me not to worry about a thing; he'd make all the arrangements. That was a load off my shoulders. Then, a dear friend in Hanau, Germany called and told me he would drive my car to the port at Bremerhaven, and ship it home for me. This was another major concern of mine. All was done and now all I had to do was go to the Rhein-Main airport.

The day before we left, I decided to take the boys out to eat, since all our furnishings were on their way to the States. Unbeknownst to me, it was a German holiday and everything, including restaurants was closed. I had walked these sidewalks many times and there was no shop there. All of a sudden, I heard these metal chains rolling up right near me. And there, right next to us, was a pizza parlor. I am not lying or stretching this fact. I had never seen this restaurant before, though I had been by there countless times. I stood there with my mouth gaping. Not only did the Lord provide a meal for us, but He gave us our very favorite, "pizza". To this day, I cannot explain where it came from, but the Lord wanted to show me ahead of time that He alone was my Provider. I learned a new form of trust that day, and little did I know what He had ahead for us, but I did learn that absolutely nothing is impossible with God. And He can provide for us, even if all looked bleak. As long as I have trusted Him, He has been faithful to provide for my every need.

The reason Jim had the asthma attack was to move him to Colorado, where he ended up retiring. It was there he was called to pastor, and we settled down after the Air Force. We didn't know what God was doing, but He sure did. We had never dreamed of settling other than in one of our hometowns. How we have loved these years though.

Simply, Supernatural: Part II

When Jim was six months from retirement in the Air Force after twenty years of military service, the Lord began to put things into place for Jim's call to the pastorate. Jim's asthma was better, but it wasn't completely gone.

The first thing the Lord had to do was to work on me. We had built a nice home in Colorado Springs where Jim was stationed at NORAD, under the mountain. He liked his work and we met some great friends. We loved our home and Colorado. The kids were happy with school. As far as we were concerned, we were home at last and were through with moving for the rest of our lives. WRONG!

We were members of First Southern Baptist Church, Security-Widefield. During an invitation, they were singing the song "Ready to Go, Ready to Stay".[5] I'll never forget the turmoil I was going through. It was a question God was asking me and I couldn't understand why. After all, we were as settled as we had ever been. So, I pushed it out of my mind, but that didn't work. I felt I was being torn apart. Finally, I said in my heart, "Well, I sure don't know why You are asking me if I'd be willing to GO, which is what I think You are asking me. I will go if You told me,

---

[5] Palmer, A.C. "Ready". Composed by Tillman, Charles D. Published in 1956.

'BUT'....At that moment, I was flooded with peace. He said, "That's what I wanted to hear." I still couldn't understand so I never said a word to a soul. I just decided to WAIT, and SEE.

During our last six months in the Air Force, God was dealing with Jim, unbeknownst to me, about surrendering to full-time Christian service. He didn't know what type, but since he was Educational Director for a very fast growing church, he felt it would probably be that. Our pastor had been speaking to Jim about needing a full-time Education Director position.

At that time, if you were retiring from the Air Force and going into a new line of work, they could put you in for what they called *Operation Transition.* The Air Force would continue to pay you and you would go into your new job for six months to train you for that line of work. Since Jim had been in the electronics field for the last ten years, this fell under this program. No one, including Jim, thought he'd get it. But, God thought differently. He was paid his regular salary for the next six months, while he worked full-time for the church. Still, Jim had a feeling that this was not what God was dealing with him about.

God made it clear near the end of the six months that He was calling him to preach. He told the Association Missionary and he turned Jim's name in to Florence, Colorado to fill the pulpit, while they were searching for a new pastor. Jim and I both felt totally befuddled, unqualified, and scared to death. We knew God could perform miracles, but this would have to be the biggest He ever did if He could make a preacher out of Jim and more if He would make a preacher's wife out of me. Anyhow, I had never played the piano, and every pastor's wife I'd ever met had played the piano. HaHa!

When Jim preached in Florence it was his first sermon ever. After the service, the Pulpit Committee asked if they could consider him for their pastor. He quickly told them he was going to put in his paperwork to go to seminary. A month later, they called him again to fill the pulpit. At the end of the worship service, the Pulpit Committee formally extended him a call and told him they felt strongly he was the man who was supposed to be their pastor. They added that they could care less if he had gone to seminary or not. Jim ended up accepting the call, as he just knew this had to be of God.

To make a long story short, we sold our house. The day we were moving from Colorado Springs, to Florence, we had decided we needed to be on the field, so we were moving, whether the house sold or not. We had eaten lunch with an elderly couple who owned a small ranch. I had made the remark what a great place that would be to raise boys on, since the river was right down the lane and they could have animals. Little did we know they would call us back before our house sold, and told us the Lord told them they should sell their place to us?

We didn't know they had already planned to move back to Missouri. We had a good laugh and told them first of all, our house had not sold, and even if it did, we couldn't afford to buy theirs. The lady asked me if I remembered the remark about it being a great place to raise boys. I remembered, and told her I never thought she would connect that to us. Then they told us to move in, never mind if the house didn't sell, we would settle up and adjust the price when we sold our house. In the mean time, it would be rent free. Now if that isn't supernatural, I don't know what is? While in the midst of moving to that home, when our house was in the worse condition with boxes all around, the house sold. That couple who sold the house to us, did exactly what they said they would. And our wonderfully blessed boys got to live on that country lane down to the river for six wonderful years. We knew if God could do this, He could do anything.

Our six years of ministry was dotted by one miracle after another. The people in Florence were wonderful. It grew from around 45 people to over 250. On special Sundays, we had over 300 people in Sunday school. God rose up some of the most godly men and women and we had some staff members that caused churches all over Colorado to envy us and wonder how we got such gifted men. We got each supernaturally. I believe with all my heart that it was as close to the ideal churches, described in Acts, as there was a love, unity, and fellowship that drew people. Jesus was the center of all that was done. The Holy Spirit's power was obvious. There was bold preaching and teaching, souls were being saved, and Christians grew and grew and grew. People gave 20% to the church, so we could call staff members or build new buildings needed for the growth. Once we could put them in the budget, we did, and people had been so blessed by the giving they asked Jim to give them more challenges. They had seen God work supernaturally in their lives and wanted to see it again. They couldn't praise God enough. We were though a simple little church in the top ten in baptisms several times in our association. How could this be? It was God. He found some nobodies, who He could work through.

Some people have tried to give the credit to Jim, but let me tell you, the people who made up this church family will tell you, it was God, not Jim Royal. Interestingly enough, Jim was called back here after it had nearly been destroyed by the flesh, and God brought it back to a dynamic church. It not only was Jim's first, but also his last church, he retired in 1995 from this church.

When Jim was sent as a church starter in Glenwood Springs, Colorado in 1978, our house in Florence came out for sale around 4 P.M., and it sold around 4:30 P.M. When we left Glenwood Springs a little over a year later due to the oil shale boom fizzling out, people told us we'd never sell our house, as the bottom had fallen out of the real estate market. They didn't know our God. We sold our house in a little over a month, and made a $10,000 profit, and sold it by owner.

After we left Glenwood Springs, we were called to a new work in Cripple Creek, Colorado. When we moved to Colorado in 1968; we had made a day trip to Cripple Creek, an old gold mining town. It was so dilapidated I asked Jim what kind of people would live there. Little did I know that when we moved from Glenwood Springs, we would be the ones living there? Jim was the first full-time pastor there where we bought and restored an old church and redecorated it. We spent three years there and loved it.

From there, we moved to Colorado Springs to a Southern Baptist Church. It was badly in debt due to mismanagement by the staff. The fellowship was so bad one lady told us they had to hold their legs to keep from kicking one another. In seven years the building was paid off; the fellowship was as sweet as can be, even though it was a multi-racial church. God truly did a work there. I could go on and on. How great is our God. He loves to do the impossible, when someone will let Him. I am so glad He is my Power Source.

From there we went back to Fremont County, where one of the missions we started called Jim after the pastor committed suicide. The church grew so much we had to either re-locate, there was no room to add on any more, or jump start the mother church by taking half the congregation to Florence, thus making it possible to stay in that location. They chose the latter. When we left with half the group, we took half of the building fund for ministry. It worked great and both churches once again grew.

Later, after Jim retired and the church suffered a decline, Jim was asked by a pastor friend, "Do you think this church can ever be what it once was?" Jim answered with a question. "Is God still alive and as powerful as He always has been?" That is the answer today for all our churches who are struggling to stay alive. If we will just let God do it all, and obey whatever He tells us to do. HE Can!

Simply, Thank Me
(*That's Enough!*)

Some years ago, our Associate Pastor asked us to spend Thanksgiving with him, his wife, and their little girl, who was quite grown up for three years old. When we sat at the table, her daddy asked her if she would like to pray. She eagerly volunteered. Here was her prayer. "Thank you Lord for the turkey, and thank You for the potatoes, thank You for the gravy, thank you for the dressing, thank you for the peas, (here she peeks at the table and goes on) and thank you for the cranberries, and for the tea. Amen."

Now, as sweet a prayer as that was, God would've been happy with a simple 'Thank You Lord for our wonderful meal'. What I am trying to highlight is the many words we often use when we, as adults, pray. We are taught to be specific in our prayers, but many times, we get quite wordy. The truth is sometimes we spend so much time with idle talk; we fail to find His perfect will in the matter, and hardly ever listen to His side of the conversation. I used to pray all the time for our country to back up Israel if anyone attacked her. I was very distraught if I thought the U.S.A. would side with any Arab country against Israel. Then in my devotion time, I heard a still small voice as I was praying that said, "Have you noticed that I alone fought for Israel in the past? Have you ever noticed it never depended upon who was allied with her or not. **I WAS SUFFICIENT!**

And so, do not concern yourself about what countries are with her, **I AM HER PROTECTOR.**"

What an eye-opener for me. Then, I realized even though I teach about prayer, I don't always pray as I should. Oh, yes, I need to take my family's needs before Him. But He knows their true needs so much better than I do. Why am I so interested in dotting all the I's? Why do I endlessly have to list them for Him? Matthew 6:7-8, (NKJV) says, "And when you pray, do not use vain repetitions, as the heathen do. For they think that they will be heard for their many words. Therefore do not be like them. For your Father knows the things you need of before you ask Him."

Prayer is such a lengthy study, there is no way I can do justice in these pages to mention all that is involved in it. Most Christians have spent more time studying about prayer, than they have actually prayed. So, I am trying to make this as simple as I can:

1.   Prayer is communication with God. If most of us would confess, we will admit to most of the talking. Praise Him for Who He is and what He has already done.

2.   The best way to communicate with God is to couple your prayer with reading your Scripture.

3.   Pray as He reveals to you whatever He wants to say. You may be surprised at how much He has to say.

4.   Have a certain time, a special time, to meet with Him. Better if that is before you start your day. Your day will go smoother.

5.   Ask God to help you with your prayers, as God knows your true needs.

6.   Don't limit your prayers to me, myself, and mine. Reach out to the known needs of others in your church, your pastor, church leaders, your country and its leaders, Israel and the world.

7.   Believe God is omnipotent, omniscient, and omnipresent and nothing is too hard for Him.

8.   Ask God to work through you each day. He is sufficient, and He will make you sufficient. Keep a prayer journal to write your answers to your prayers. You will be astonished at the end of the year when you look back at how many of your prayers have been answered. SIMPLY THANK HIM, AND MEAN IT.

Many an 80 year-old and older has grieved over their inability to minister as they did when they were young. I always explain when I get the opportunity, that life has different ages and stages. Today, their ages can change their ministry to a ministry of prayer. They don't have to be able to walk, plan, prepare, study, visit, and go to meetings. You can even be bedridden. YOU SIMPLY PRAY. What could be more important to your church and family than that? What a powerful need today!

Simply, True Love

Again, Song of Solomon 8:9, (NKJV) says, "Many waters cannot quench love, nor can the floods drown it. If one were to give for love all the wealth of his house, it would be utterly despised." Many have found that this is as clear a statement as could be made of **true love**. Love is eternal and absolutely nothing can kill true love. 1 Corinthians 13:7a-8b, (NIV) says, "True loves always perseveres, and never fails." Unfortunately, what our world calls love, is not love at all. A good illustration was when a preacher spoke to our youth. He said to his teenage son announced to his dad, "Dad, I'm in love". His dad turned and looked at him and said, "Son, you aren't in love, you're in lust."

Too many times, people interpret emotions such as lust for love. We as Americans add to the problem with our wrong interpretation, or use, of the English language. We, as a nation, are being "dumbed down," especially with our vocabulary. Everyone has the ability to use whatever "active" vocabulary that is practical for their area of life. But, we should have an "inactive" vocabulary where we know the true definition of many more words than we used each day. From that storage, we should draw when necessary, and use for the best description of whatever we are talking about. The word that should be used today in place of love is one we use when speaking of chocolate, Mexicans, sports, music, arts, etc. You could say I like these things very much. But love is a very different word.

The best description of this word is found in 1 John 4:8-10, (NKJV) which states, "He who does not love does not know God for God is love. In this the love of God was manifested toward us, that God has sent His only begotten Son, that we might live through Him. In this is love, not that we loved God, but that He loved us and sent His Son to be the propitiation for our sins."

God is the epitome of love. It is not just one of His characteristics. He is love. Look at His life. He demonstrated that love over and over, and He still does. He was willing to let His only Son die in our place, so we could accept His forgiveness and receive His gift of grace, eternal life. John 3:16, (KJV, emphasis) says, "For God **so loved** the world, He gave His only begotten Son, that whosoever believeth in Him should not perish, but have eternal life." This is real love. It is eternal and it doesn't depend upon our performance, it is eternal. It will give everything for that love, including life itself, if necessary.

Measure this up against the "so called" love a person who "loves" for what he can get in return. Examples are for security, sexual attraction, or self-gratification, political position, social status, etc. You get the picture? How many times have you heard the statements, "I fell out of love," "I once loved him, but he killed my love," "How can you still love someone who has changed so?" "I'll just get a divorce if our marriage doesn't work," "I've been married four times, and I've loved all my husbands." I hate to tell you that does not describe true love, as I know the definition of *true love*.

A new phenomenon took place over the years my husband was a pastor in regard to marriage ceremonies. Marriage vows were pretty standard and contained words such as I will love, honor, obey, and cherish in sickness and in health, till death do us part. Then, candidates for marriage started to ask if they could write their own vows. Many today don't want the old vows, because they don't really mean them, nor do many intend to follow them. Time hasn't changed, as much as people have changed. Their interpretation of love has changed.

We know that love sometimes means changing a baby's *poopy* diaper, cleaning up vomit, their messes, their clothes, etc. But what about when that macho man or that beautiful woman ages and needs not only their dirty diapers changed, but the *poopy* trail into the bathroom or their vomit they no longer can clean up by themselves. This can happen at any time due to illness, accident, or perhaps Alzheimer's disease. That, yes that, can only be done when one's love cannot be quenched or drowned. Having true love doesn't make it easier, no one said it would. But folks that is true love. It cannot be killed, it gives till there is nothing left to give, even life itself.

Yes, true love is eternal, unconditional, and hardly even notices when others do it wrong. In other words, it is never historical, bringing up all the times one feels they were wronged by their mate. 1 Corinthians 13:4-7, (NLT) says, "Love is patient and kind. Love is not jealous or boastful or proud or rude. It does not demand its own way. It is not irritable and it keeps no record of being wronged. It does not rejoice about injustice but rejoices whenever the truth wins out. Love never gives up, never loses faith, is always hopeful, and endures through every circumstance." This is *true love*.

Slavery

We hear much about slavery today. Personally, I thought that was all in the past. Let me say up front, I never had even the tiniest bit of racism in my body. For one thing, I was born and raised in Massachusetts. The little town I grew up in had only one black family. I don't even know why they were such private people, but I doubt I even saw them more than four times in my lifetime. Whenever I saw them, I asked my Mom about them. All I can remember her saying was that they were very private people. That wasn't very unusual in Massachusetts, as there were a lot of white people who stayed completely to themselves and didn't fellowship with anyone, other than family. I do remember her adding that all people were alike and since God loved them, we should too.

In high school, we had studied much U.S. History, so I had heard about slavery in the South. Since I went to a large high school, it wasn't unusual to have a black student. And that is what we had, one black girl. Our school was large, since it included several towns in our county. She was a well liked cheerleader, and sadly, she died of bone cancer while attending our high school.

Since we also had an Air Force Base in our county, we had a Southern boy. His name was John, and we called him Johnny Reb. We all liked him, as he was very outgoing and full of fun. We just couldn't understand the Southern culture he spoke about at all. We simply laughed at him when he told us how it was in the South. That was another world, and to us, it was as foreign as China.

Then I married a Southern *red neck*. They say opposites attract each other and we certainly were different. It wasn't until we married and moved to Georgia outside Savannah to Wilmington Island where his family lived, did I really get a good look at what a racist was. It was all around me, yet, I still couldn't understand some people's deep-rooted feelings. Black people were everywhere, but totally segregated.

Jim's family was divided concerning blacks. Jim had grown up sixty miles from Savannah in a rural, sparsely populated community. The only playmates he had were black, as there were no others his age. With the added fact that he went into the Air Force, which was integrated, he never was into racism. Nor were the other Christians in his family. But some held on to their hatred of blacks and do to this day. His dad thought they were fine, just so they stayed in their place.

Through the years, we saw a great transition in the South. It wasn't always an easy road, but we felt proud that finally people were no longer being judged by their color. Yet, we saw a new phenomena arise, reverse discrimination. This was due to some of those who hung on to their prejudices, and felt blacks were being favored over whites, not their receiving equal opportunity. Then after a while, that even seemed to disappear. Blacks had made great strides in their education level, entering every profession and being accepted. Racism was definitely disappearing.

It hasn't really been worse, until the last seven or eight years that the coals of past slavery have been fanned and come to a full flame. None of these blacks have ever been enslaved, but they have been used like pawns to do what others with wrong motives have manipulated them to do. You see, most young blacks are enslaved, yet not to white slave owners. They are enslaved to drugs, alcohol, gangs, and the government hand-outs to the destruction of their lives. Their great-grandparents who loved and trusted the Lord, some even under bondage, would turn over in their graves if possible. They wouldn't believe where their descendant's so-called freedom has taken them. You see, the very worse slavery is the slavery to sin.

What all African Americans need, and I have had many Christian black brothers and sisters in the Lord Jesus, is true freedom. John 8:36, (NIV) says, "So if the Son sets you free, you will be free indeed." The greatest freedom is freedom from self and the self-life. Our African American brothers and sisters are such wonderful people and their culture is such that it should never change.

One of the greatest things that come from the exchanged life is the desire to love all people. Recently, when the white supremacist shot and killed nine people in Charleston, South Carolina, we saw the love that comes from God through Christ through family members of those killed. These people showed true Christian love and character. This is the equality all of us should be seeking. Let's pray that those who have been deceived, distracted, and detoured from the right way, God's Way, will come to the Lord, experience true freedom, and be delivered from destruction.

Sometimes, We Get So Deep, We Sink

One thing I have loved about Billy Graham through the years is that he always kept his messages simple enough that no matter who was listening, they could understand the simple truth. I know some men minister to the super educated, who love the eloquence put before them. In fact, it is their natural communication and God sends a man who meets their need, and can be greatly used of God.

Most churches; however, have all types of people in attendance. A person who is extremely educated can understand a pastor who preaches the simple truth. That doesn't mean the message is not deep, but it is delivered in such a way that all people present can understand it. This is a true gift.

What if a poor soul wandered into a church where the pastor used $100 words to preach the same message, and the visitor is lost at sea throughout the whole message? Oh, I'm sure most of those there would be impressed with his educated delivery, but had it been clearer all, included this poor soul, would have gone out rejoicing.

In my husband's ministry, we have had people with P.H.D.'s in our service regularly. They were humble and encouraging to my husband. I felt like they were some of the most spiritual Christians I had ever met in my days. There was never a time when they didn't grab my husband's hand on their way out of church and look him right in the eye and tell him that God had spoken to them during the service and wanted to thank him for the message. One such person was a psychiatrist and the other a retired university professor.

My husband would've been so intimidated if they weren't such an encouragement to him. All they knew was that God had placed them both there. Even though Jim didn't near measure up to their qualifications, they were brothers in Christ who came to hear from God. Jim never changed his vocabulary for anyone. Acts 4:13, (NKJV) says, "Now when they saw the boldness of Peter and John, and perceived that they were uneducated and untrained men, they marveled. And they realized that they had been with Jesus." They knew Jim had also walked with Jesus.

Today, some pastors try to preach to the educated, mostly to impress them with their knowledge. They flaunt their education caring not if any there feel they do not measure up. They are so deep that the people sink, when the *simple truth* would be sufficient. It is so amazing that few of them ever see the failure of this and wonder why they never get called to a church where they feel they could preach to their equals. No one seems to ever see their potential.

Perhaps, there is a message in that. If a man has his eyes on a big church, he probably will never get one. But, if he is just faithful in the little things, God will give him greater things. If you are a valuable worker, faithful where you are, God sees you and will reward you either in this life, or in the next.

Spiritual Gifts

Added to the many differences in my husband Jim and myself, due to our backgrounds, are the differences in us due to our different spiritual gifts. Jim has a strong gift of prophecy. Not the foretelling of future events like Old Testament prophets, but the forth telling, or proclaiming, of the Word of God. I think it would do well if I write a little about the gifts we have.

One of the aspects of Jim's gift of prophecy is the desire to point out sins through his proclamation of the Word of God. This causes others to see the sin in their life, and it causes them to repent and accept God's gift of salvation through faith in His Son Jesus Christ. Romans 6:23, (NKJV) says, "For the wages of sin is death, but the gift of God is eternal life in Christ Jesus our Lord." When preached from the pulpit, or speaking one on one, if a heart is ready to accept this, it is as sweet as music is to the ear.

Often, though, it is carried into the home, as it was in Jim's case. He was constantly pointing out to our children the flaws in them. And when he was tired, he could be quite harsh in doing this. Certainly not like a person with the spiritual gift of mercy. One with this gift would have difficulty disciplining their children. If they did discipline them, they would do it with much mercy, and empathize with them, often too much.

Now, I have the spiritual gift of teaching, which means I have a drive to teach the Word of God. Not only this, but I love the research, planning, and preparing, as well. This is merely the Holy Spirit doing all these things through me, as I clearly recognize. He is my Power Source. To make it a little bit more opposite to my husband, I have a very strong secondary gift of mercy. I have had a hard time, at times, teaching a lesson knowing someone in the class thought I'd prepared that lesson just for them. Because it was my call, I still taught it, despite my feelings.

At home, when our children were still young, it was so hard for me to be silent when Jim corrected the boys. I actually went into our bedroom and wept, because I couldn't stand to see the boys spanked. Of course, if I had done the disciplining, it would have been tempered and with my merciful nature, or probably not done at all. I have to tell you even though I agreed the boys needed this discipline; I would have handled it quite differently. Today, I realize Jim was right, as his boys still think he is the greatest, and have told Jim they should have gotten more spankings than they did, for they deserved more than they received.

What I wanted to share is how even our spiritual gifts affect our make-up. They are a part of who we are. So they affect our life at home, as well as in church. When I fully studied them, I began to understand why people act the way they do. Yes, our personalities, our temperaments, and our talents affect our daily lives, but so do our spiritual gifts. Romans 12:4-8, (NKJV) says God gives us different gifts as He wants, and that they are to equip the saints for the work of ministry in the church. Ephesians 4:7-8, (NKJV) But, we show them in everything we do, and we can't choose the one we like, God does as He sees fit.

How I wish Jim had the gift of exhortation then. He would have encouraged our boys and me more. But, I realize now I needed a prophet, and my strong-willed boys also needed a strong dad to correct and make them do the right thing, at times. I also realize, now, that even the churches we ministered in needed a prophet spirit, not a softer, gentler pastor. Yes, there are a few who balked at his firm leadership, but the proof was that God blessed greatly, and many were saved under his leadership. One thing was sure, everyone knew he loved them. Like my boys, they knew down

164

deep one reason everything went so smoothly was due to his firm hand. And no one doubted his strong faith and the fact he always gave God the credit for all the success we saw.

God always sent the servers we needed and they loved to serve. They served out in the community as well as in the church. People like me, and others, who didn't have this gift to meet the practical needs of others, didn't have to feel guilty about spending their time in their own gifts.

We never lacked the givers. Whatever the need, they rose up and gave much beyond their tithes. How could we have done all we did without them. We were able to pay cash for two building additions, and later added a big gym and paid it off early due to givers in the church. At the same time, we were able to start two mission churches. One large church Jim pastored was gravely in debt when we got there; and I said earlier, in seven years, we paid off the whole church and it was debt free. We were even able to hire staff members by people giving 10% above their tithe. Then, as soon as our budget could, we paid them from it. At one church, we had stepped out on faith so much, that when we went back to giving only a tithe, people said they missed giving more, for they were blessed so.

This is the absolute truth, and it is a testimony of what God can do when the spiritual gifts are at work in a church that simply trusts God to do what He has always promised to do. Many times, people want to give credit to the pastor for such great accomplishments, but even to this day, Jim always sets them straight. There is no limit to what God can do when we simply take Him at His Word. God hasn't changed, unfortunately churches have changed. He is just waiting to do it again.

Flesh vs. Spirit

If you have raised, or are presently raising children, you surely have noticed that you have to teach them to do right, yet they automatically know how to do wrong. Like touching that which you told them was a no-no. (Even looking at you first, to see if you are watching.) What about the first time you put them down in a church nursery? Not having been around children before, what a shock when that little darling of yours goes up to another sweet little one and bops him on the head. Oh, then how about the time you got home from the mall and found out your little boy had stolen a pencil, telling you they'd never miss such a little thing?

That was that old sinful nature he, as well as we, inherited from Adam and Eve in the Garden of Eden. Once saved by grace through faith in Jesus Christ, we then have come alive spiritually. (Ephesians 2:8-9, NKJV) Yet, we learn quickly, even if we are stronger due to God's power in us, we constantly must battle with the old nature. The only difference, is when we call on God's power, we can stand against it. (2 Corinthians 5:17, NKJV)

Choices have to be made, resulting in either blessing from obedience, or curses from disobedience. Curses really are the end results of our own disobedience. (Deuteronomy 30:19-20, NKJV) But, we can be sure God will use all for His good, which is His good. Simply put, our Lord told us challenges were coming. They reveal our lacking in any area; we need to work on, or to test, the depth of our trust in Him. I realize spiritual growth takes a lifetime. If we think we are mature, we aren't. He will certainly reveal this to us, as we battle with the old nature.

I have often thought I was mature in an area, only to fail a test of God. This showed me my lacking of maturity. Do you look at other Christians and think they need to grow up in the Lord? Be careful, that is one of the attributes of a mature believer. They do not concentrate on others behavior; rather, they are constantly trying to improve their own actions.

Remember, if a person is a non-Christian, he or she is acting quite normal. Without the Holy Spirit empowering us, we are incapable of acting within the constraints of the Word. They simply do not understand what we are saying or doing. (1 Corinthians 2:14, NKJV) says, "But the natural man does not receive the things of the Spirit of God, for they are foolishness to him; nor can be know them, because they are spiritually discerned." Not until they accept Christ, and receive the Holy Spirit into their lives, will they begin to grow. It takes a lifetime of growth for a person to realize all that God expects of them. That is, if a person wants to live under the unlimited power of God.

Finding a Pastor

Churches, flocks, have different types of people, just as men called to shepherd these flocks are different. It stands to reason that a *one fits all* is not going to work. Only God knows who would be best to lead different sheep, (people.) As you look through the Bible, you see God has used many different types of men. Some were very educated, some not educated. They were simple fishermen, a doctor, and a tax collector, so it behooves us to realize that we cannot choose a pastor the same way we would hire a CEO. Yet, that is what is happening today.

For the following reasons, I feel I can comment on this most important topic. I was married to an Air Force man and at that time, we were active members in different churches, each time Uncle Sam moved us. After he retired from the Air Force, he was called by our Lord to be a pastor, thus I got to see both sides of a pastor's life. After he retired from full-time pastoring, I got to go with him as often as I could get away, where he filled the pulpit for other pastors when they were on vacation. We also did volunteer mission work in Mexico in an American Community Church for eleven years. During this time, I got to observe much of this subject from many spectrums. It is from this background, which I write.

Jim's first pastorate was in a little log church in a small town made up of ranchers, a lot of prison guards, and mostly non-professional people, though we did eventually reach some professionals. This doesn't mean all young pastors are sent to these small towns to begin with. How foolish it would be for all of us to think God always works the same way. Isaiah 55:8-9 makes it clear, "God's ways are not our ways, nor His thoughts our thoughts." He chooses Whom He wants according to what He intends to do with both the pastor and His people. Since only He knows what His intention is, only He knows who would be the man for the task.

It isn't how the candidate appears to be, fat, skinny, has a small family or has a large family, educated, non-educated, experienced, or has no experience, eloquent, or not the best speaker. IT IS ALL OF GOD. God can do whatever He needs to do through whomever He wants to do it through. So, we must, PRAY, PRAY, PRAY, for His guidance to find His will in finding His man. All else depends upon this, so it is very urgent.

Let me say, God isn't against organization, nor am I. It is very sad to see a church flounder, because there is no order and does not know where to begin. But, just remember, all the best organizations in the world will not help you find God's man for your church. Nor is a resume a guarantee you can tell all about the man.

The first thing most people do when their pastor has resigned is to form a Pastor Search Committee. Unfortunately, most churches do not begin with Prayer, which is where all important decisions should start. Then, they will often have an opinion poll vote. "Who would you like to elect for our Pastor Search Committee?" WRONG! Then, the next poll taken would be to find out what type of pastor they would like to lead them. WRONG!

Generally, someone will suggest they get an associational leader to come and give you counsel and train you where to start in your selection of a pastor. Much assistance can come from these associational leaders, but God help you if he majors on the same ways to hire your pastor as you would a professional leader, or looking at your church needs and decides he has a buddy looking for a church that would be just what you need. If you have the right help you need, he will major on the spiritual methods, starting with prayer.

I have been interviewed as a potential pastor's wife, and my husband has been as a future pastor. It is wonderful when you get to see God working despite a committee. Jim has been told, "We tried to get everyone, but God wouldn't let us get anyone but you." That, plus what God had told him, sure affirmed that he was God's man for that church.

I have had the opportunity to serve as a member of two Pastor Search Committees since Jim retired as a pastor. I would like to share a little of what I encountered. One particularly stands out as what could have been a nightmare experience. First, I would like to share a few things I believe should not be asked by a candidate for pastor to a Pastor Search Committee. Then, what if anything, a pastor should, or should not ask of a Pastor Search Committee. A question by a candidate can tell you a lot about him:

1. How much of a salary are you offering? Who is really going to pay your salary? God or the church? A pastor should know this. It doesn't matter what the church will pay you. Where is your faith? Don't you believe God can stretch your salary and you can live better than a person who makes more than you? Once Jim had proposed we take a step of faith that he felt the Lord was leading him, so we were having a question and answer time in a business meeting. One of our deacons, a charter member of this church, arose and said, not nicely, "Well pastor, I just want you to know that the first thing we do in this church is if we get in a bind, is to cut the pastor's salary." I knew when Jim answered immediately like he did, that God was speaking through him. Jim said, "Brother, I want you to know, that neither you nor this church pays my salary. God has always paid me well. And that doesn't enter into this decision at all." The church unanimously voted to take the step of faith. And our deacon learned a lesson about using money to control his pastors that day.

2. What will you expect me to do as your pastor? This raises a red flag. Can I not get a word from God? Are there things that I won't do if asked? Do I have a servant spirit?

3.   What do you expect my wife to do? Why? Does she have limits to what she will do?

4.   What hours do you expect me to work. There again, will you only work a 9-5 day? What if you are called out at midnight, because an old man loved by his wife and daughter just shot himself in the head, as he couldn't bear his suffering another second from emphysema? My husband was, and he even cleaned the brains off the stoop that the emergency techs left, so the man's loved ones wouldn't have to do it. It was near zero degrees that night.

5.   What can I expect from my deacons? Deacons are not to rule the church, they are servants set aside to meet practical needs, so the pastor can devote his time to the spiritual matters of the church. A look at Stephen and Philip in Acts might give you a glimpse of what character traits a deacon should possess.

6.   Am I expected to visit church members? Well, what do you think?

7.   Are you as a church in debt? When we went to Colorado Springs, we knew they had nearly lost that beautiful church because a staff member mismanaged the church's funds without the church's knowledge. They had to personally borrow money to pay off the church debt. If that would have kept Jim from going there, they would not have paid off that church debt and seen many miracles in the seven years he was there. Jim knew of their financial bondage before he went there. Why did he go? God told him to.

8.   How many tithers do you have? None of your business. That is between them and God.

9.   Do you have any wealthy givers? Actually, what you could discern from that is "I'd sure like to know, so I could always please them. In other words, I'm a man pleaser not a God pleaser. Only one thing is necessary if you go to a church. Is God calling you to go there? Tell them why you sense He is calling you.

Yes, a question from a candidate to your committee can reveal a lot about him.

Also, some good questions from the candidate to the Committee that can be asked are:

1.   The most important question you should ask is… "What led you to consider me as a candidate?" (Prayer hopefully.)

2.   Do you to feel God is calling me to be your pastor? Why?

3.   What is the spiritual life like of this church? This doesn't mean if it is very low you wouldn't go there. Sometimes, God sends us to this type of church to take this church to a higher spiritual level than they are now.

4.   What would you describe as the Power Source of this church? The perfect answer would be the Holy Spirit, but they could have several answers. The bottom line would be it is ALL OF GOD.

5.   What part does prayer play in this church's life?

6.   What is the most significant step of faith you feel this church has taken?

7.   Do you have a prospect file? If they do not, you need to tell them why you asked them. Each name represents a soul. If they are not interested in reaching out, tell them you are. If there is not a marriage of this church and you, check back with God and make sure He is calling you there.

It is better to be honest up front. It is of utmost importance that you tell the absolute truth and so should they, whichever side you represent. Please do not assume that a person is telling you the truth. I told the last Pastor Search Committee I served on not to tell the candidate what you want in a pastor. Ask them good questions, let them answer them, and ask the Lord to show you the truth. If you tell the candidate what you want, all too often, he will tell you just what you want to hear, in order to get the job. This is especially true if you have a large, growing church.

One young man said after I told them that, "I don't believe a pastor would lie, or that he would not be dishonest with a Search Committee." Oh, how I wish I could have told them that he was right. I saw it with my own eyes, heard it with my own ears, so I know it is true. He was young and very naive. We were as careful as we could be, and our pastor candidate misled us and he was so good that we didn't pick up on it until later. When a man asked about elders says he doesn't care what a church decides about elders, that he has been in churches with them and without them, and he says he doesn't care one way or the other. Then, he begins in less than a month after being voted in as pastor inserting all the reasons we need elders and tries to implement them, despite the church having decided long ago they didn't want them, and told him their constitution stated that. There is a problem. That same church had to ask him to leave in a little over a year, because he would not accept the churches stand. That was not the only thing we found out he misled us on. But sad to say, it does go on in churches today.

Be sure he gets a copy of your Constitution and By-Laws, so he will know who he is joining, not the other way around. Tell him if he cannot agree to them, he might be better going to another church. Let him know much prayer went into the forming of such rules for your church and you would stick by them.

Many a pastor has been known to pick a few men to rubber stamp all his agenda. That is why prayer is so important. That is why electing the right men and women for your Pastor Search Committee are necessary. It can take anywhere from six months to a year to get a pastor. But without God's guidance, leading you to the man He wants to lead you, all is for nothing. I am convinced that so goes a leader, so goes the church. If you have all the ingredients in a New Testament church that the early church found in Acts had, you will have the same results. God will add to the church such as should be saved, and saints will grow and serve with joy. Yes finding a God-called pastor is a tough process. But it is an important one. SIMPLY PRAY, PRAY, PRAY. God wants you to be led by His God-called pastor as much as you do, or even more.

Spiritual Maturity

The journey of my life has been a long one. When I think of all the travelling that Jim and I have done in our married life in the Air Force, I hardly can believe it was possible. So much travelling was done by me with three little boys in tow. I thank God we were able to go with Jim on his new assignments, but when going overseas, the children and I would not follow until a few months later. Now that I look back, I wonder how we did it for so many years. Only through God's sustaining grace was it possible.

My spiritual journey also has been a very long one. When I think back to my early days as a Christian, I realize I have gown immensely, but I have had so many failures along the way, as well. Even today, as I am tested sorely with Jim's health issues and my own declining strength, I often feel like I take two steps forward and three back. Only with God's hand on my life is it possible to go on.

As a young Christian, I prayed I would grow like Paul talked about in 1 Corinthians 13:11, (NIV), which says, "When I was a child, I talked like a child, I thought like a child, I reasoned like a child. When I became a man, I put the ways of childhood behind me."(I would put childhood things behind and go on to be a mature servant of Christ.) I must confess I had no idea how God would bring that about. Many of the adversities of life were used in shaping my life to bring me to where I am today. It seems they were needed to bring me to total trust and reliance upon Christ. One could overlook a serious health problem thinking it was only growing pains. This happened to my middle son once in Germany. Jamie would wake up crying with pains in his leg. When I would take him to our Air Force clinic, the doctor would diagnose the pain as growing pains. This went on for a year, and finally the doctor sent me to Frankfurt to a specialist. When arriving at our appointment, the "trained eye" of the surgeon spotted the tumor in his leg. It was inside his femur, (thigh bone). He was flown to Walter Reed Hospital where they removed a benign tumor. If not removed, it could have done severe damage to his leg.

God is like that "trained eye" the specialist had. His "all seeing eye" sees those areas in our lives that need to be cut out. He uses circumstances to remove serious flaws that could eventually lead to great harm in our spiritual lives. I have had many such surgeries in my physical life, but many more in my spiritual life. I would never ask another Christian to evaluate my Christian life. Only God knows my heart, so only He is worthy to do this. His mercy, compassion, patience, and love temper the anger, while He is at work refining me. He is sufficient in all things and I can rejoice to know He is not through with me yet. I can count on Him continuing the process until He feels I am who and what He has intended me to be. Through reading His Word, He spotlights those areas I need to "cut out" or give close attention to. The result is spiritual maturity.

Hopefully, if a person is older, he is wiser. He is more mature spiritually, is deeper in the spiritual principles and disciplines of the Christian faith. This would prepare him to face the challenges of getting old. The challenges that come with old age can be great. One man said that old age is not for sissies. He certainly knew what he was talking about.

God may be merciful and call one home like our dear friend who simply dropped dead after he completed his favorite past time, a round of golf. We had another who we had said for years she would die working in her yard for she worked there daily, and rigorously. She never went to church that she didn't bend over and pull a few weeds. How did she die? In her back yard digging up some old trees. It didn't surprise us at all.

Actually, both were doing what they loved to do when God called them home. But, many more go through long bouts of suffering from cancer, or some other ailment that tests their deep faith. This is a much harder road to travel, but our merciful God can pour out His grace and through this suffering, can teach others how to spend those last days here on earth. What we have to ask ourselves is whether we are truly mature and able to face any and all adversities in the future, as God uses our life to teach others how to live and die.

God's grace is sufficient, but we must appropriate it. He never told us it would be easy, life just isn't always easy. But, Jesus never gave up when He was called to die on a cruel cross, too much was at stake. Nor can we give up, for others are watching and too much is at stake.

Test of a True Sunday School Teacher

If someone right now tried to take my Sunday school class from me, I'd fight. Why? Because I think it's mine? "No!" Because I feel God has placed me right where I am, not man. I know God uses men to do His will, if any acknowledge Him. But, I've talked with God a long time, I know when He is speaking and I know He has called me. He began to close the door I was in, while He opened the door wide that I was to go into. He began to show me how He was putting things in place for me to teach there.

When I got there, a young woman came to me and said, "You are an answer to my prayers." I asked her to share with me why she felt that way. She said, "You see, I have been asking God to send us a Ladies Sunday school teacher to teach us what we are hungering to know, and you are the answer. This was a great affirmation, even though I already knew I was where He wanted to do a work, and I simply joined Him. I have learned so much from the Lord as I have been teaching ladies. God has shown me much through the years, through the positives and the negatives of what it takes to be a godly Sunday school teacher.

The first thing I learned is you **don't grab a brand new Christian and put him or her into a teaching position, of any age group**. That's what happened to me when I first became a child of God. I didn't know anything about the Bible, how could I teach others? I needed desperately to be taught, so I told our leaders I was floundering, and couldn't handle where they had put me. "Please," I said, "let me go into a Sunday school class, so I can learn." What a joy, when I was where I needed to be. I was like a sponge, I soaked every word up. How many people have just dropped out of church, because they couldn't handle teaching, and didn't know how to say what I did? They didn't want to leave, but also didn't know how to handle the situation.

The second thing is **not all older Christians are called to teach**. You will never make a person with the gift of serving into a teacher. A server has the drive to meet the practical needs of people, and he or she is good at it. Why would you try to force a square peg into a round hole, when you have an abundance of round pegs? It doesn't work. When our church studied spiritual gifts, Jim had a public school teacher come to him and share that she loved teaching school, but absolutely had to make herself teach a ladies class. Jim told her to quit, and pray and find out what she was supposed to do in our body.

To give a great illustration of the foolishness of this was when our pianist came to Jim and said she had wanted for years to play the organ, but we had an organist, so she didn't want to hurt her feelings. To make a long story short, while talking to the organist, she said she wanted to play the piano for years, but was scared to tell anyone for fear she would hurt her feelings. He shared the foolishness of the situation, and you never saw two happier ladies when they switched instruments. Both experienced true joy.

A wise pastor studies his people and finds what area of service they love and serve well in. Then, he gives them jobs accordingly. You discover your givers pretty quick. They are the ones who are the first to give when any need arises. They are compelled to give, give. Some have had to put their houses and cars in their mate's name, so they couldn't give them away. What would we do without these givers? Why in the world would you want them to do anything else if this is what God wants them to do? This applies to any spiritual gift in the body of Christ, the church.

Another person who should not teach is the **unprepared, uncommitted teacher**. Jim was an Education Director at a church we attended when he was still in the Air Force. A man in the men's class kept coming to Sunday school and would hand the teacher's quarterly to a man and say it was his turn to teach that day. When Jim approached him about it, he would try to resign. So Jim would ask him to stay. Jim told a visiting Sunday school worker about the situation. Very quickly, he told Jim the next time it happened, to take the quarterly, tell him thank you for his service, and find a God-called Sunday school teacher who would never give his responsibility up so easily, and would be committed to those he taught. How well I know that today. I love my class, I pray daily for that class, I ask God to grow that class and make them usable to do God's will. I pray God will use the teaching in this class to grow each and every lady He sends to us. I pray they will be all that God wants them to be. I pray that I will just be a microphone, and God will teach through me. That is why I could never quit. Only one person could cause me to give up my class, God Himself. And He knows how to tell me so.

Another unprepared teacher is the **rabbit chasing, yakker**. Week after week, month after month, these teachers shoot the bull, and play around. The one thing he does not do is teach the lesson. He might read a statement then ask what the class thinks. After Jim retired, we visited a church and they had one such teacher. How that pastor allowed this man to stay in his position, I'll never know. Jim would have fired him in a minute. He would both go and learn how to teach the BIBLE, or else quit. This may sound harsh, but could you do anything else? Doesn't that person know he has a calling of God to give an in depth study or what message the lesson has for the class. Study time is not fellowship time, where everyone comes together to share their week's activities and joke around.

Don't all teachers know that he or she must be absolutely committed to praying for and preparing for their class? This includes being ready to answer any questions the class may ask. Don't teachers realize their responsibility is to God, not just to the class and the pastor? The God of the universe holds him or her responsible. Don't they care? James 3:1, (NIV) says, "Not many of you should become teachers, my fellow believers, because you know that we who teach will be judged more strictly." I can't even imagine how one could treat such a holy calling with such contempt. You say, "Well, he's just ignorant, he doesn't really mean anything by it." For gosh sake, no wonder the churches are dying, no wonder we have a world full of baby Christians, who live like the devil and are living exactly like the lost world. They even vote for men who will destroy our Christian foundations. It drives me crazy!

While this is going on, young men and women who have come from godly homes, taught right from wrong live compromising lives. They should be mature enough to teach others, but often, they aren't even in church. You see, they are out playing at skiing, fishing, 4-wheeling, hiking, climbing mountains, surfing, or soaking up the sun. My neighbor built a big storage building out back of his house for his toys. I told him I liked his new *toy box*. He just laughed. It is all a game. While all the while souls are going to hell. Forgive them Lord for they don't even know what is happening. Unfortunately, one day, they will.

"The Great I AM"

In Exodus 3:14, God said to Moses, "I AM WHO I AM." God is **Whoever** we need Him to be. There is absolutely nothing impossible for Him. He becomes whatever we need Him to be. He meets our every need, because He is the **Great I Am**.

He tells us He will never leave us or forsake us. I am your Creator. I am your Protector. I am your Provider. I am your Problem Solver. I am your Prayer Answerer. I am your Promise Keeper, I am your Savior. I am your Security. I am your Power Source. I am your Guide. I am your Teacher, I am Faithful, I am Truth, I am Love, I am Eternal, I am Merciful, I am Compassionate, I am your Good Health, I am Wisdom, I am your Hope, I am Discernment. I am Worthy, I am the Living Word, I am your Spiritual Gift, I am your Daily Sustainer. I am these, and so much more.

How can we know and believe all these things, yet not call upon Our Lord and not avail ourselves of all that is available to us through Christ? Could it be that it has never been more than head knowledge, and has not got into our hearts? You do not ever have to worry about Him giving you something that would not be good for you. Especially if you have prayed in His will, not yours.

I believe one day our Lord will ask us why we did not call upon Him more often when we were in need. Would we hesitate if our earthly fathers were able to give us anything we asked, and he had promised to do just that? Some believe we can't take those small things to Him for we should only call on Him when the difficult things come. In other words, He isn't concerned about the small things of life. He is too important to care about these small things. I have searched and searched, for a dropped contact lens, then prayed, an instantly, I found it. Others think just the opposite, they hesitate asking Him to do the miraculous or meet our great needs, thinking we would be presumptuous. I have asked God to sell my house when no other houses were selling, and He sold it when others did not sell. How ridiculous this is. He has told us in Jeremiah 33:3 to call upon Him and ask and He will answer. And again, in Jeremiah 32:27. He wants us to recognize who He is and there is just nothing too hard for Him.

The longer we walk with Him in an intimate relationship, the more we realize how much He loves us and is always available for us to come to Him and ask what we will. Also, the longer we walk with Him; we realize how much He loves His children and wants to demonstrate to the world His Power. How else will they know just what the benefits of the Christian life are?

No, He isn't a grandfather who we can push into doing anything we will. Our heavenly Father absolutely will not give us anything that would harm us. That is how much He loves us, and our love for Him doesn't allow us to ask anything of Him that we truly do not need.

I love my children. I would do anything I could to help, and not hinder them. But I would not give to them anything that would cause them to become lazy, become ungrateful, or lead them astray. Even if it hurt to see God have to deal with them when I could easily write a check, I would not enable them to do wrong. I believe God treats His children the same way.

We must remember in all of this that at times, He allows suffering and grief to come into our lives, though never without purpose. Adversity, problems, comes to show us He is able to give us GRACE. He knows some things we will not know until we have been tried and purified by fire. We call that *tough love*. We know it is good for us, because it works. I have walked a good many years now with Him, and I can testify that He knows what He is doing, even though I have not always known. He is worthy of my trust.

I am glad God is the **Great I Am**. I am glad He has an unlimited supply and there is absolutely nothing impossible with Him. In the book of John we see Jesus made some claims using "I Am," claiming to be equal with God. Jesus is able to do anything God can, as He is equal with the Father in all things.

The High Cost of Public Education

The high cost of public education today is the LOSS OF INNOCENCE. Innocence is of great value. Once lost, it can never be regained. Education can be achieved at any age. It can be postponed and can be recaptured, even when one sets it aside for long periods of time. Having worked with Adult Literacy, I have witnessed men and women who couldn't read or write learn this skill rapidly, and go on to lead very productive lives.

Once, I spoke with a lady who was raising a child who was a genius. (He entered college level when in elementary school.) I shared my concern for the poor situation my own family was in, having a very intelligent child of their own. Quite surprisingly, she said to me, "An intelligent child will always learn, even in a bad school." I also asked her about her child's diet, as I had seen him eating Oreo cookies and milk for breakfast a couple times.

She said, "He has always eaten this for breakfast." So much for the notion, that if we don't give our children the right breakfast, they cannot perform well in school. Even severe physical limitations or harm can be restored, but INNOCENCE cannot. Even sold-out Christians, some of them pastors, have testified to the curse of their addiction to lust and pornography.

The greatest tragedy today in public schools is in the lives of children that are losing their innocence at a very young age, and it brings long-range consequences. Not many people have seen the videotape of the interview of James Dodson with Ted Bundy, the night before Ted's execution, but for those who did see it, they know that he traced his perversions, and road to murder back to his innocence looking at pornographic magazines as a young boy.

The reason we have so many Christian schools today, and many are home-schooling is for this reason. One, these are not perfect, and definitely they can bring problems. But these problems can be resolved, and excellence regained. INNOCENCE CANNOT BE REGAINED, ONCE LOST. One of the goals of Christian schools and home-schooling is to build character and teach the need of morality in all areas of life. As I look back over my childhood, one of the things I cherish most is my memories of the blessed joy of innocence, unscarred by filth, foul language, lewd acts, pornographic materials, or groping. My parents fought for my innocence, sending me to a Catholic school for elementary and junior high training. Even though I found I was definitely taught much about church laws, not basic Bible truths, God led me later to receive that training.

Education and sports, though important in our children's lives, are not on an equal footing with spiritual training and protection of INNOCENCE. Most Christian schools were started to provide a refuge from a world full of "smut," and a place to educate and build character in our children, according to God's Way found in His Word. This is in direct opposition to public school philosophy. We are given the command to train up a child in the way he should go, and when he is old, he will not depart from it. (Proverbs 22:6, KJV) In other words, don't let the world train your children in the ways of the world.

But, you say, not all Christians go that way. That is true, it is a personal choice. But, we have the responsibility to teach them the right way, and the choice is theirs. We can lay a foundation of truth for them, and they have a choice between the two. There was a time when public schools agreed with homes and churches. That is not true today. Just look at the mockery students must put up with today, not just from students, but teachers alike.

Recently, a high school in the next town had a crisis. It seems most in the school had been found to be taking pornographic pictures of their naked bodies and sending them to other students, including sport stars on their cell phones. It was so widespread that when discovered, it made the national news, papers, and T.V.

One doesn't have to wonder how shocked their parents were. In our state of Colorado, to do this if to be found guilty could mean a lifetime of having your name on a permanent sexual criminal listing. Can you even imagine the long-term consequences of this? Not only in applying for entrance to a college of your choice, limiting your choice of jobs in the future, but also rejection of society in general. I cannot tell you of all the fallout this has brought to these parents, trying to see to it that they were disciplined, and yet weigh that against the future consequences, harming them their whole life for a stupid indiscretion as a foolish youth.

The saddest thing of all is the fact that their INNOCENCE is forever gone. They may regret the stupidity of the act, but the damage is done. The question we are faced with today is, "IS THE HIGH COST OF PUBLIC EDUCATION, THE LOSS OF INNOCENCE, WORTH IT? Will my child have to fight the attacks thrown in this area their whole life? Like a computer, what you put into your mind can be called up anytime by the attacker.

The Simple Truth About "Church Hopping"

To those who often go from one church to another, known as "Church Hoppers," let me ask you. Did you leave your former church under the leading of the Holy Spirit? Or, are you so intolerant that you run every time someone, or the body, has angered you or disagreed with you?

One of the greatest problems in our modern day churches is that we are losing credibility in the world. I recently heard a person say that Baptists are known for their fighting. Surely not Lord! We had been known as far as I can remember as a people of the Book (Bible). We have even been called "Bible Thumpers". That is surely better!

What I truly desire if for us to be known as true Christians who preach the whole counsel of God, and act like Christ, whom we love and serve. That we love all people like God does, not ever seeing them as what they are, but what they can become transformed by Him, like He does.

If there is anything I have learned, it is that like people, churches are different. In our very mobile society, it is not unusual for a person to move miles from our home church to another state, another culture, and at times, they even speak an unknown dialect, example Georgia or Alabama from New England.

Please, don't try to change them into your home church. Remember, you are the guest, you joined them, and it rarely works anyway. Ask God what He desires from your life now that He has placed you there. We all have something God wants to develop in us and to use us to grow others. It takes time, love, patience, concern, and prayers. If you wait on God, He will work circumstances where you can discuss with them how they could improve their church in a way you wanted to share early on and it, simply, wasn't the right time.

In all our years in the Air Force, we moved around the world, and constantly, we were in many different churches. You see, Jim and I didn't have time to check out all the churches to see if they suited us. We just found the closest Southern Baptist Church and joined it. We found fellow Christians from all over the world. Talk about people being different. What we had in common though was we were all away from our home towns. We knew we had a talent to share, needed a family away from our own, and probably would be moved from there to heaven only knew where, by Uncle Sam.

Some of the most wonderful Christians we met in these churches. True friendships were formed. The fellowship was wonderful and we all grew spiritually. Though we were all different, from different parts of the world, we majored on the positives, prayed about the negatives, and left the rest with God. Though we were all different, especially where rank was concerned, we all were a church family, and didn't care about the differences.

Many times, Jim and I missed our dear church family when we left, who we often got closer to than real family, only to find a new church when we moved and built the same kind of relationship. Oh, if all our churches could feel the love we had for each other. The ties that bound us were unbreakable. Acts 2:1, (NKJV) says, "When the day of Pentecost had fully come, they were all with one accord in one place." All together means more than a place, they were in one accord, in one mind, especially spiritually.

You will never build this church family atmosphere, unless you are active more than just Sunday Worship hour. When you go to Sunday school, you will get to know people better. But, the best way is to have them in your home. It takes somebody to start if this isn't going on in your church. Maybe, you could be the first. And don't quit just because you are not invited to their home right away. You would be surprised at the number of women who cannot cook today. And you cannot imagine the people who have phobias when it comes to having someone in their home. Just show them how by the way you keep inviting them. One day, you might find out you started a new trend.

The True Meaning of Christmas

As we come to this blessed Christmas season, it would do well to remind ourselves of what Christmas is really about. You truly cannot take Christ out of Christmas, for it would be nothing without Him.

I cringe each time I hear that the Christmas tree is a religious symbol. Decorations of a Christmas tree originated in Germany. Along with the many other worldly symbols such as mistletoe, holly bells, etc., these trees are purely secular traditions and do not represent what Christmas symbolizes.

Now, I am not saying that a Christian cannot use these symbols or have them in their homes. What I am saying is that they, along with Santa Claus, a tradition started from St. Nicholas was brought here by the Dutch, and this tradition must be completely separate from is the true meaning of Christmas.

Christmas is a spiritual celebration. It represents God intervening into history and sending His only begotten Son into the world. Yes, He was born to a virgin named Mary who was betrothed to a man named Joseph. On a lonely, dark night, God burst into history and sent a bit of heaven to earth in the form of a baby, so that He could reveal God the Father, and save the world from sin. He did this by letting His Son be a substitute sacrifice in payment of our sin debt in full.

Jesus was not sent to be born in a king's palace, though He was the King of kings, and Lord of lords. No, God sent Him to be born in a humble stable, and He was laid not in a bed of lace, but a manger for His bed. Only love could work this out, so none of us would ever doubt that we were included due to our status in life.

Yes, when you see a Nativity set in the midst of all secular symbols, or hear a beautiful Christmas carol, though this is getting harder and harder to find, remember, this is the true symbol of Christmas.

I look back as a child, and have fond memories of all the traditions and fun activities we celebrated at Christmas time. But, I thank God I came from a family that made it very clear that the real Christmas story was read to us. We went to church to hear this story again and again. It breaks my heart when I see families, stores, schools, and even churches discarding the true history, religious symbols of Christmas. How very sad, indeed. In times like this, we need our faith for these desperate days. Jesus is sufficient. Thank God for His birth. (Luke 2:1-20, NIV)

There is Nothing Simple About Grief

Grief is a complex thing. It has many faces and definitely takes on many forms, depending on the person. It comes to the lost, it comes to the new babe in Christ, and it comes to the mature Christian. Jeremiah certainly knew about a type of grief that had nothing to do about death. Jeremiah 9:1, (NKJV) says, "Oh, that my head were waters, and my eyes a fountain of tears, that I might weep day and night for the slain of the daughter of my people!" He grieved over those living in sin.

Jesus also suffered greatly under a load of grief. Luke 22:44, (NKJV) says, "And being in agony, He prayed more earnestly. Then His sweat became like great drops of blood falling down to the ground." It wasn't a grief over someone else's death, but of people's response to His upcoming sacrificial death. It seemed no one understood what was ahead for Him, even though He grieved over men's sin to the point of dying for them.

What a message for our time. Grief over sin! How many parents, grandparents, and great-grandparents are grieving over the sins of their family? This world, a large portion coming from our own nation, is corrupt. Our cities are corrupt, our schools, especially institutions of higher learning are corrupt, our movies are corrupt, our music is corrupt, and even authors who have never written trash have joined the corrupt crowd.

Many of our churches are merely institutions of apostasy and corruption. It must make our Lord want to puke. (Excuse my English.) Many in our own family, which now includes four generations, that once served the Lord whole-heartedly, now speak negatively about the church and have fallen away. What grief! There has not been a lack of prayers on their behalf, nor is there a lack of answering on God's part. But they, as well as so many others, have taken their eyes off of God's greatness, and have dwelt on the negatives. With the busy lives they have, it definitely is the easy way.

Satan has taken advantage of their vulnerability and they are unaware of how far they can fall. Oh, what if they were to call for God's grace and power to change the church. After all, God still uses the church to witness of His saving grace. What would happen if rather than complain, they jumped in and were determined to change those negatives into positive appeals? Could that be the very reason THEY were placed where they are? Oh, how this would be so much better than joining forces with the enemy, many times totally unaware.

This is a greater grief for one to handle than death. For if a child only lives half their life for goodness and God calls them home, you have the comfort of those left behind that your child had a part in pointing men to You and Your way. Lord, give us grace to remain faithful to the end in this corrupt world. No matter what, let us labor with You to change our churches, not criticize the church that You died for.

As far as grieving over the death of a loved one, 1 Thessalonians 4:13, (NKJV) says, quite simply, "But I do not want you to be ignorant, brethren, concerning those who have fallen asleep, lest you sorrow as others who have no hope." We are not told that we should not grieve. And grief comes to each quite different when they lose a loved one to death. But what He says is that we are not to grieve as the lost world grieves. I know of a lady who has been grieving over a child for over thirty years and has convinced herself that this is normal. If she knew this verse, and claimed it, she would not still be grieving.

Walls of Protection

God's laws are walls of protection around us. They have been given to us, because of His great love for us. Before each and every commandment we should insert, "Because I love you, you shall, or you shall not…" We all recognize that an inventor of a new technology or product knows more about the benefits and dangers of those products than anybody. So, it shouldn't be too surprising that our Creator knows more about His creation than anyone else. Anyone who can speak all into existence surely knows what is best for that creation. And we know that all other inventions start with God's created materials.

Why then do we listen to the most ridiculous theories of fallible man over our Almighty God? Over and over again, He is proven to be Who He claims to be. If anyone has an honest heart and an open mind, God will and does reveal Himself to them. You don't have to be a brain surgeon to recognize fire burns. It is simply common sense to know that if you make $20,000 a year and spend over $30,000 a year, you will eventually end up in bankruptcy. You may use credit cards to postpone this, but it doesn't take a degree in finance to simply figure out it will catch up with you sooner or later.

Why then, do we believe the lies that men tell us today? I am appalled as I watch newsmen ask men and women on the streets questions that the average junior high school student knows the answer to, but they are completely ignorant of. But if asked about a movie, or about a movie star, they can answer with no delay. Yet, many are now, or have been to college. Are we so in love with knowledge, that it blinds us to the evidence? 1 Corinthians 1:25, (NIV) says, "For the foolishness of God is wiser than human wisdom, and the weakness of God is stronger than human strength."

Many today live in the greatest country in the world, yet they fail to recognize it. People still come here from around the world for medical procedures, because we have the best doctors in the world. People will, and do, take advantage of our medical technology. Yet, we have let men attempt to destroy this medical system attempting to bring us to where less blessed nations are, who envy us.

We could feed the world with what we waste. We are told we must yield all our resources to enemies who declare openly that they want to destroy us. What kind of stupidity is that? We ignore our friends around the world, while helping our enemies. This is especially true in giving them weapons to destroy our faithful friends, and eventually us. We waste God's resources He has given us in abundance and listen to men who convince us we will run out if we don't let them, not God, tell us how to ration them. If only these "so-called" brilliant men would check history, they would find out the only time God didn't take care of His children's needs is when they disobeyed HIM.

Environmentalists tell us that a sucker fish takes priority over irrigating food products, all the time getting richer and richer off products they recommend. God tells us to care for His world, but it takes an idiot to believe these people who ban us from using the resources God has provided for us. God has blessed us with oil off our shores, yet no one will use that oil for fear of depleting our supply. If God has given us this oil, and He let a widow's pot of oil never run out, why can't He do that now? 2 Kings 4:2-7, (NKJV) says He can, He would continue to do so if we would only believe Him and not the idiots. I have to agree with the man who said we have become so open minded that our brains have fallen out.

It is so much easier for me to recognize our God is in control of the universe He created, and uses this very nature to discipline those who think they know more than He does. After all, WHO gave them the intelligence they have? Once a lady in one of my Ladies Bible Study groups gave her heart to the Lord and was burdened that she had never thanked God for His marvelous provision through the years. So before eating with her family, she announced that from now on, she would like to thank God at mealtimes. She bowed her head and thanked God. Her husband, who was not a Christian, said, in front of the children, "It's me you should be thanking. I provide the food, shelter, and clothes with my good job, not God." What a foolish man indeed! In less than a year, this man was confined to bed with crippling arthritis, so severe he could no longer work. You see, our good health, abilities, jobs, and everything come from the Lord. Without His blessing and His provision, we are nothing. And He can revoke them anytime He wishes.

I once prayed asking God why He didn't intervene in a certain situation, like I knew He could. In a still small voice, He spoke to me and said, "Time is short, I will settle all accounts very soon. There is no reason to act now."

If we chose to follow the idiotic thoughts of today, those who think they are so great, rather than follow the common sense God has given us, well, that is your God-given choice. "But as for me and my house, we will serve the Lord." (Joshua 24:15b, NKJV) The benefits and the consequences are eternal and I have tested all Biblical truths over the last sixty years, and they are true. "Jesus said to him I am the way, the truth and the life, no one comes to the Father, except through me." (John 14:6, NKJV) He is not one of the ways, He is the way. I do not use the term *fool* thoughtlessly; it is simply in the Bible that says in Psalms 14:1, (NKJV): "The fool has said in his heart, 'There is no God.'"

Many today say Christianity is solely one of the ways. This is foolish, indeed. One of the things they hate mostly about Christianity is they claim we are exclusive. They want us to join in with the rest of the world. They claim that because we hold to our beliefs, we are right wing radicals and we are wrong. Well, their disagreement is not with me, it is with Almighty God. I hate to tell them, but they are fools if they think they are mightier than the God of the Universe.

Wasting Time

My husband and I don't agree on many things, other than doctrine. One thing we do agree on though, is our getting angry when a pastor gets up in the pulpit and wastes God's precious time, when he should be preaching the Word of God.

It would be better for a man to get up and simply read verses from the Bible about a topic and not even comment on it at all, than to waste the time he has to proclaim it. One way a man does that is to "warm up the members" before preaching. He usually does this by telling a few jokes or generally talking about nonsensical things. Of course, he spends ten to fifteen minutes doing this before he touches his sermon spending ten minutes in the Word.

Another way is using illustrations until he has little time left to talk about what the spiritual applications are to these illustrations. Yes, our Lord used everyday illustrations from life to describe deep spiritual truths, adding clarity to what He was teaching. But usually the illustrations were never longer than the spiritual truth itself. I have seen my husband since retiring, listen to such a man preach, rant, and perform for twenty minutes and then quickly preach the main point. I can see the fires of anger inside him being stoked. I can wait until I get home to vent my anger, but he has very little patience when it comes to abusing a man's anointed call.

We both agree that wasting God's precious time is a sin. When a person comes to hear a Word from God, he deserves to hear just that. If he wanted to hear a comic, he ought to go to a comedy theater. I want to cry when I have prayed for a person to come and get saved, or revived, only to get the person there, and have the pastor *play act* from the pulpit.

Another problem is when a pastor wastes his time with object lessons that could be taught in the kindergarten Sunday school class. He follows with a short kindergarten level message. I am all for teaching the deep truths of God simply. But when the children are in Children's church, what about the adults who are waiting to be fed meat and are merely given milk?

This pertains to preachers and teachers. My husband and I have always taken these words seriously. What greater responsibility can one have than to be entrusted to preach or teach the Word of God? He or she should take this awesome, exhortation to heart. When a man stands in the pulpit, he should proclaim "thus says the Lord," and add as little clarification as necessary. The Bible certainly can speak for itself, so why should we spend all this time to clarify it? The Holy Spirit is dealing with a soul and He is the one who convicts, not man. 1 Corinthians 1:21, (NKJV) says, "For since, in the wisdom of God, the world through wisdom did not know God, it pleased God through the foolishness of the message preached to save those who believe." Let God be God. Despite man's foolishness, men and women are still getting saved. Thank God!

Jim and I pray for our pastor daily, you should too. I pray he will preach the whole counsel of God, and not be a man-pleaser in his messages. I pray he will not play in the pulpit, nor perform. I pray he will simply let go and let God. Kindergarten preaching produces kindergarten decisions. As junk food is not good for your body, so junk food sermons do not produce healthy Christians. Could this be one reason our churches are full of babies?

Time is short, we need men and women who have been prepared to reach the Gentiles to be saved before the Rapture. Please preachers, and teachers, proclaim the Word today, even if it isn't popular. 1 Timothy 6:20-21, (NKJV) says, "O Timothy! Guard what was committed to your trust, avoiding the profane and idle babblings and contradictions of what is falsely called knowledge—by professing it some have strayed concerning the faith. Grace be with you. Amen."

How sad it is that the biggest churches often preach what the people want to hear. Yet, they never mention the controversial areas of the Bible for they want people to feel good when they leave the service. Showmanship is also a relatively new thing that is added to our services to appeal to those who watch T.V. regularly and it appeals to their carnal nature. I fear we will lose our battle against sin in the new generation coming up, as preachers are swayed by people's desires, not what God says. 2 Timothy 4:2, (NKJV) says, "Preach the word! Be ready in season and out of season. Convince, rebuke, exhort, with all longsuffering and teaching. For the time will come when they will not endure sound doctrine, but according to their own desires, because they have itching ears, they will heap up for themselves teachers, and they will turn their ears away from the truth, and be turned aside to fables."

I hate to say it, but there are churches, which to my knowledge have never preached against homosexuality, immorality, divorce, abortion, marijuana dangers, etc. Yet, our society fills T.V., magazines, books, newspapers, etc. with stories and articles, and hollers that anyone who does not join the masses in agreeing to these, what they call freedoms, are radicals and should shunned and the houses of God that forbid the participation in such evils. What has happened to our land, our preaching? It is sad.

Weary From Well-Doing

Have you ever been weary from well doing? I have been. I have been this as a wife, as a mother, grandmother, and great-grandmother. I have especially been this way as a pastor's wife. You see, we pastor's wives often have to get the ox out of the ditch. Especially if your husband is a small town pastor, and almost everyone already has a job and you seem to have to fill in just until the Nominating Committee can find a replacement. How long that will take depends upon a lot of variables.

Of course, you already have your God-called place of service, or two or three. Why do you do it? But, who else will do it? So, you slip into that place of need, minister to your husband, your children, and of course the emergency needs that your husband brings home, plus house guests every once in a while. Are you getting weary? Well of course you are! I have been too. I have talked to friends who also are pastor's wives and some have just about come to the place they didn't think they could go anymore. Can they or I quit, of course not. No, too much is at stake to quit.

You learn a lot from those times. I learned how to say no, despite the need. And I knew I had to. Satan would love to get me so burned out, that I would run away. Think what that would do to one of the churches God placed us at.

Guess what. The Nominating Committee or some other one found some round peg and got them to go into a square hole until they could find God's called man or woman. Sometimes, it takes that to wake people up to the need. As long as you fill the slot, no one else will come forward. I've even seen the actual one that was called come forth and surrender, because they couldn't stand to see a person do it that shouldn't be in there. What I want you to know is that God did give me grace during those times, I made it through and I didn't even have to complain.

Once, I was pretty overwhelmed at church when my son called from across the mountains. It was important that someone he and his wife could trust would take their six month old son and keep him, as his wife was ill. We were about to start our very large VBS the next day, and I would have him the whole week. I knew the need was great, and my son who had a very demanding job, could not take off. I simply said if you can just get him here, I would be delighted to take care of him. Believe it or not, I got through it, despite the inconvenience. I found God already knew my need of grace, and it is sufficient in all things. And I really enjoyed having my sweet grandson. I learned I could do all things through Christ who strengthens me if I would but ask Him to do it for me.

Now, I am 78 years old and feel, at times, I am doing too much, for Jim is getting older too, 82 now. He can't always help me. But there is too much at stake for me to quit. I have found out that I can do a lot more than I think I can do. I want to teach all our Lord has taught me. I want to share His wonderful attributes. Just lately, I am seeing so much fruit from areas of service that bless me and others. So, I'll keep on going until this old body won't go anymore, at which time, I pray the Lord just lets me simply come home.

A little footnote: My husband died one month before he turned 83, February 13, 2016. I cannot tell you how many people, who upon hearing of his death could not believe it. They would say things like, "I just thought he would live forever, because he was always on the move, teaching, preaching, or just ministering." He spent his years as a faithful servant. He never lost his love for souls, and I felt he would witness to anyone who would just stand still and listen. He did this even in the hospital before he died. He never wasted time or words. What a role model to be married to!

Jim, like Paul, was called of God and it made a difference. Ananias, in Acts 22:14-15, (NIV) said to Paul, "The God of our fathers has chosen you that you should know His will and see the Just One, and hear the voice of His mouth. For you will be His witness to all men of what you have seen and heard. And now why are you waiting? Arise and be baptized, and wash away your sins, calling on the name of the Lord."

I believe when God calls you, it makes the difference.1 Thessalonians 5:24, (NIV) says, "The One who calls you is faithful, and He will do it." That is a promise that you can stand upon. His grace is available to do anything that is His will. When we struggle the most is when we let others manipulate us to do those things He has not called us to do.

What Do We Do?

When members of a church leave our fellowship, yes, sometimes mad, what do we do? First of all, let me say there is absolutely no competition in the Lord's work. At least, there never should be. Are we not all serving the same God? Have we not all benefitted from His precious gift of salvation? (John 3:16) If God is love, and we are His children, should we not have His traits, which include loving all people unconditionally, and persistently?

Should we not want to sacrifice for others, including the unlovely, since Jesus sacrificed His very life for sinners? If He washed the sweaty, dirty feet of His apostles, should we not be humble enough to admit we are not always right and everyone else wrong? Even some pastors say, if not verbally, by their actions, "It's my way or the highway." How then can some say when others leave, "Good riddance?"

How many have left a church because a Sunday School Director changed their room? Or how about fought and lost in a vote over the color of new carpet or new curtains in the sanctuary? How many have left a church, because of a building program? No one ever said they had to give such and such an amount. If they didn't feel led to do it, the pastor didn't want them to give. Yet, they left.

What would happen if people just remained in a church, no matter what? I have to tell about a man in one of our churches. He was a chartered member of our church. In other words, he had been there since the formation of this church. He was a member of our church council, made up of all the leaders in every part of the church. They met once a month and voted to proceed or not in matters of church business. Then, they would present to the church business meeting any matters they agreed on, for their vote.

Despite whatever type of business to be conducted, this man gave as many reasons that could be given why we could not undertake this. He never did this in anger, never was unkind, he just debated against any and all business. However, after it passed, this man would never leave the meeting mad. Would he move his membership to another church? NO! He would grab everyone's hand, give it a hardy shake, then go out and support whatever the action, just like he had recommended it personally.

I learned to love this man. Even though I felt at the moment I could strangle him, there is no doubt he was a true Christian. To this day, I wonder if he just played the devil's advocate, so we could contemplate the negative side of every bit of business we handled.

But, I did find out he had a bit of a problem spending money when I served with him on our Day Care Center's Committee. After arguing with him for an hour over giving our Day Care workers a 25 cent an hour raise, I was quite frustrated, as was the whole committee. These workers had volunteered to work for less than the minimum wage until the church could pay them more, once it started growing. My husband overheard us as he passed the room, stuck his head in the door and said, "Call for a vote, you've had plenty of discussion." We did, and he was the only negative vote. As usual, he supported us 100%.

I would never want to serve on another committee with him, but, oh how we need people like him in our churches. This was his church; he loved everything about it, and was actively involved and always did business with love. He died in his 80's, still working in this church many years later.

Would that all members felt about their church like this man did. He may have disagreed vehemently at times, and said what was on his heart, but never quit loving his church family. If all the people who have left churches for whatever the excuses could feel like this man, how different the end results would be. I'll never understand no matter how many years I live, why people leave their church home over such petty problems. Not only that, but then go on the phone and contact others to convince them they ought to join them. The only one who gets hurt is the Lord, and those who joined these people, carrying on this scheme. I pray we will all wake up before it is too late. We have enough attacks on the church and Christianity today without this. I am not your enemy, nor are you mine; our enemy is Satan.

We share a wonderful Savior; let's not waste precious time that should be spent telling the Good News, for time is short. Love has always drawn people, and love will still draw people. One of our greatest downfalls is that the church is known for their fights. This drives them away. People are desperately seeking love. 1 John 4:20-21, (NKJV) says, "If someone says, 'I love God,' and hates his brother, he is a liar; for he who does not love his brother whom he has seen, how can he love God whom he has not seen? And this commandment we have from Him; that he who loves God must love his brother also."

What Does it Mean to Be Saved?

Just what does it mean to be saved? Many people wrestle with this question. Is it just walking an aisle in church and repeating a few words led by the pastor or some other counselor? What is one saved from? What is one saved for? Is there an age one must be before one can be saved? Is there an age we can reach whereby we are too old to be saved? What about death bed conversions, are there any real ones? If God is love, how could He send anyone to hell? Why do I feel saved sometimes, and at other times not feel saved? Why do people say that I must be saved before I can understand the Bible? Why do people get so upset when a person mentions they are a Christian? What does God expect me to do once I am a true Christian? These are all genuine questions that one asks. Let's answer these questions as simply as we can.

Simply put, true salvation is being born again. Once, we were born physically from our mother's womb. We are born again, a spiritual birth, when we believe with all our hearts that Jesus is the only begotten Son of God and offered His life a sacrifice to pay for the sins of the world. You can read the 3rd chapter of the Gospel of John and it is explained as simply as can be. Also, 2 Corinthians 5:21, (NKJV) says it all. "For He made Him who knew no sin to be sin for us, that we might become the righteousness of God in Him." God placed the penalty for all of our sin upon Jesus, and took away our penalty for said sin, and gave us His righteousness. One is saved from what we deserved, hell. We are saved to live for Him forever.

Many say, "I've led a good life." "I try to treat others right." "Why am I a sinner?" And the Bible says all have sinned, either by thought, word, or deed. (Romans 3:10 and 3:23, NKJV) If you haven't done any wrong, if you thought about it, or said the pettiest negative remark, you can recognize you are a sinner. You don't have to be the instigator, but if you agreed to someone else's doing wrong, you committed sin. For to break even a small part, is to break all. James 2:10, (NKJV) says, "For whosoever shall keep the whole law, and yet stumble in one point, he is guilty of all."

What we earn for this is spiritual death. Romans 6:23 says, "For the wages of sin is death, but," it didn't stop there. It goes on to say, "the gift of God is eternal life in Christ Jesus our Lord." Grace is a gift. We earn spiritual death, but God gifted us with eternal life. This is salvation.

God demonstrated His love for us by letting His only begotten Son die in our place for us. This means, He became our substitute and paid the price in full. Now, I am just (as if) I'd never sinned, (just/as/if/I'd, justified). To just walk an aisle in church, sign a paper and say we want to be saved simply is not salvation. It could be we do this because we are operating on emotions. Unless we realize we cannot earn it, buy it, or inherit it, but only Christ could pay the price, and gift us with it, one is not saved.

When I do this, give my life in return for Christ to save me, I am truly saved forever. I have actually been saved from past sins, present sins, and all future sins. What we would have to do if we sin once saved, is what the Word says in I John 1:9, (NKJV), "If we confess our sins, He is faithful and just to forgive us our sins and to cleanse us from all unrighteousness."

Now, I must live for Christ. This means my life should reflect His image, His will, His Way, and His Word. This should be the goal of my life.

As we know, different people come to Christ at different ages and stages of their life. This is due to many reasons. First, some children come to Jesus very early in life for they have heard the message very early in life. Some have actually been in church since the first weeks of birth, in what we used to call the "Cradle Roll." Yet, some of us were much older before we ever even heard the Word God, or Jesus Christ, outside of a few times when someone used those words to cuss within our hearing. If you were not raised in a Christian home, it could mean you might not have heard the Gospel until much later in life. There is no age limit. Either young in life or late in life when God calls, that is the time to come to the Lord.

When we talk about death-bed conversions, we realize with modern day medical technology, mandates not to resuscitate, hardening of the arteries, dementia, and even assisted suicides, these leave much doubt as to more than a few getting saved on their death bed. It isn't because God wouldn't want them to be saved, it is just doubtful they would come to Him when they have rejected Him all their life, and with hardening of the arteries comes hardening of the heart. To be risk free today is the best time to come to the Lord. Confess, repent, and believe.

God is love. If you want to define love, look at His life. God has never sent anyone to hell, nor will He ever. He has done everything possible to keep men and women from going there. Technology today allows more ways for us to hear the Gospel, (Good News) that Jesus saves. We have to ignore churches, their godly members, T.V., radio, revivals, the information highway, prayers others said for them, etc. So if a person goes to hell, it is because he chooses to ignore all of the above, but mostly, he ignores God's love and provision.

As I recently read Paul's life, I marvel at what God did and what Paul endured to get to Rome to preach of the love of Jesus Christ. Better than that, when I think of God's great love for me, and what He did to lead me to Him, I marvel. Here I was steeped in Catholicism, church laws, and never heard the Good News, when He sent a Georgia cracker via the USAF to tell me and show me God's love. I am what I am today, because of His love for me.

God's Word, the Bible, is a spiritual book for spiritual people. That is why a historian, as good as he is at understanding history, cannot fully understand the Bible. He has an element missing from his understanding of spiritual truths. When we are saved, the Holy Spirit comes into our beings and empowers us. At that moment, the Holy Spirit, our Indweller, helps us to understand all truth. This is called spiritual discernment. John 16:13, (NKJV) says, "However, when He, the Spirit of truth, has come, He will guide you into all truth; for He will not speak of His own authority, but whatever He hears He will speak; and He will tell you things to come." If you read 1 Corinthians 2:14, (NKJV) you will understand why non-believers do not understand the Bible. This is why you need to be saved before you can truly understand spiritual truths. As you grow in Christ, you develop a spiritual sensitivity, which enables you to see beyond what is happening in the world. You begin to see God working through even the crises.

The reason some get so angry with Christians is there is no way they can measure up to God's standards. We don't think like they do, we see more than they do, hear what they cannot hear, and they definitely cannot stand up to our relationship with God. Thus, the world does everything it can do to silence us. They resent our disciplines, our godly lives, for they shed clarity on their own lives. Actually, if they have not made the choice to follow Christ, they are acting quite naturally. It is all about choices. We make a choice to choose God's way, and they choose to follow the world's way. God expects much from His own children, but we do not expect a child of the world to act as we do.

We just follow the tune of a different piper. I am not like the Old Testament saints, under the law. I do what I do, because I have chosen a different way of life, and I love it. If I had never met God's way in His word, and I lived the same life I do now, I would still believe this way was the best way. Just think no enslavements to alcohol, drugs, or sexual enticements. I have only had one husband, so I am happy as I have no other marriage to compare it to. I have missed out on sexually transmitted diseases, like herpes, Aids, syphilis, etc. My children have never had to wrestle with a new Mom or Dad, sometimes more than one. I do not have to share my Dad with other children though not his, they get all his time. I don't have to repair the broken pieces left by divorce. Really, I haven't missed anything. That doesn't mean we haven't had problems. But we grow through the problems.

The most wonderful part of being a Christian is to know that I am loved unconditionally, and eternally. God's love doesn't depend upon my performance. In other words, money cannot buy true love. I cannot kill God's love. No amount of money would be enough to buy God's love.

That brings up the matter of feelings. Some days, I don't feel loved, I don't feel wanted, and I feel worthless. You cannot build truth on the basis of feelings. Nor can you build your faith in God, and His Son on feelings. Feelings are deceptive. You are what God says you are. Is just doesn't matter what anyone else says. Man can mock us, try to intimidate us, put us down, say we are ignorant, lie about us, or accuse us. It just doesn't matter. My Creator, Savior, Defender, Provider, Protector, Promise Keeper, Prayer Answerer, Problem Solver, Power Source, and Lover of my soul is all I need. He is Almighty, He has unlimited power. He is Omniscient, has unlimited knowledge. He is Omnipresent, unlimited presence. He has been with me around the world and is still with me, and has promised to never leave me nor forsake me. (Hebrews 13:5, NKJV)He is sufficient. He is worthy of my all.

God has given me so many gifts, first and foremost, Himself. He gave me grace (unmerited favor) when He saved me, security of my faith, my home, my family, my friends, my church and more, His wonderful Word, good health, my spiritual gift of teaching, spiritual discernment, and so much more. What more could anyone ask for.

Yes, salvation is the first step one must take to be a child of God. He didn't make it difficult for each of us to come to Him. All we have to do is to take that first step, confess, repent, and believe with all our heart. At that time, we are saved from God's wrath, and are saved to be with Him eternally. Earth is just our temporary home. We are just passing through. Once we are saved, we have stepped into the spiritual realm, and He does the rest. We then have the promise to live with Him forever in our heavenly home. Won't you do that today? After being born anew, we are to grow up in Him. That means we are to read the Word, go to church, and find new friends if the old ones will not tolerate your commitment to the Lord. You will simply change your ways, your desires, (your want to do) your hangouts, and your schedule. Your world will change, along with all the rest of your desires.

What I Have Learned From My Negatives: Part I

One way we learn is from the negatives. We watch and realize that what we see is teaching us WHAT NOT TO DO. Like observation of a mother and very obviously we say, "When I am a mother, I will never do that." In my life, I have observed many negatives that taught me what not to do as a woman, wife, as a military wife, pastor's wife, as a Christian worker, as a grandmother, mother-in-law, great-grandmother, as a Sunday school teacher, and finally as a friend. So, my life has been filled with observations. I will share what I have learned from negatives, but will not mention names. If you think this was you, just remember, I have met numberless amounts of people in my travels, in the Air Force, in the ministry, at Revival services where my husband preached around Colorado, from conventions, retreats, etc. Once my husband and I spoke of the fact that everywhere we went we met some we knew, or knew someone in common with whom we were talking to.

As a WOMAN, a WIFE:

When I was young, I thought how limited females were. I grew up in an age where women had fewer professions to choose from. If you were a young lady, your end goal was most likely to be a wife and mother. I doubt my mother ever thought there was an alternative career for her. Most women who desired further education then were to become a teacher or a nurse.

Today, women work at every job a man does. (Could that be one of the reasons that fewer jobs are available for men?) In the subdivision I live in, the local high school carpentry program builds a new home, and sells it yearly. It is a wonderful program for those who don't intend to go to college. Now it is available to girls and boys. These workers are in great demand as soon as they graduate, as they are skilled carpenters by the time they finish four years of training. When I see the young women carpenters on top of the roof, it never ceases to amaze me. When they are young and single, it is fine. But very few can handle this work after very long, and they have children.

Another field that has more and more women is law enforcement. My son, who was a police officer for thirty-two years, saw many changes in this field. He told us on many occasions about how the physical agility test lowered their standards, in order that women could pass the test. The sad result was how it affected police work all over. Very few women could truly do the job. The physical demands out in a patrol car, plus the backup responsibilities for their fellow officers so often left the men at risk. My son said that out of all the women he had to work with, there were only three he felt he could depend upon. (In thirty-two years.) One was a former Olympian weight lifter who was as strong as an ox, and two others who were extremely fit for women. Most of the women hung back until a man was there for a call to back them up, if there was a dangerous situation. Many have to retire early, not from injuries, but from doing tasks they were never meant to do. Equal amounts of women work today as men. The roles have become cloudy. Like one man I heard in line at a grocery store, ranting to the checker, "Oh, these modern day women have degrees in everything, except house cleaning and homemaking." It was clear after a few minutes that he rented properties and just had a family move out leaving the house in a veritable mess.

What I learned from all this and more was that God wants all women to evaluate their lives, and set their priorities right. Proverbs 31 tells is that our first priority is to be a godly woman who doesn't compete with her husband, but supports and meets his needs, above all else. We may work away from the home, but our husband and children must remain above all else our first priority. If we cannot do both, the JOB MUST GO! Or in the beginning, we should have mutually decided it was best not to have children.

Is this harsh? Well, we have well documented case histories of the broken homes, broken lives, and now a broken society to teach us from the negatives. The time to be praying is before we prepare for our life commitments.

AS A CHRISTIAN WORKER:

I have met some of the most capable people in my moving around the world, many who never amounted to much spiritually. They had so many abilities, capabilities, but had no availability to the Lord. They gave all their time, talents, and tithe (money) to the world. Yet, God would raise up another person, sensitive to the Holy Spirit's enabling power who simply stood on Philippians 4:13, (NKJV), which says, "I can do all things through Christ Who strengthens me." Though he or she was very limited, they were very loyal to God and He did great things through them.

For abilities mean nothing if there is no availability. One must be accountable to God and realize their abilities were given by God for God's use, above all else. That is a reality, whether we believe it or not.

I love music. I have sat in front of people who had the most beautiful, clear voice of an angel, and I wanted to cry. Why? Because not once in years did I ever see them bless others with that glorious voice to bring people to the place of worship. Yet, at the same time others with much less talent struggled to sing, since there was no one else who answered God's call.

Once a very gifted and trained musician confided to me that she didn't really want her talents, and really never cared to use them. That was incredible to me. For when she sang, people were moved by the Holy Spirit. I sincerely told her God had truly gifted her with her talents and people loved to hear her sing, that they were blessed when she sang. Rather than touch her heart, she said, "Well, I never asked for that gift." This was a very teachable moment for me.

What I Have Learned From My Negatives: Part II

AS A MOTHER:

One of the greatest miracles of life is how one man and one woman come together and give birth to a beautiful, very dependent child. One of the greatest responsibilities given to us as parents is to raise that child for God. You see, God truly says to each mother, "I am loaning this child to you, raise him or her for Me. One day, you won't know when, I will come and take him or her home with Me." "I have a very special plan for this child, so be sure to stay in communication with Me, so I can guide you."

The rearing of three sons took a lot of loving, nurturing, guiding, patience, forgiving, training, disciplining, lack of sleep, rocking when sick, etc. What did I learn from the negatives of this experience? Boy, did I learn to pray! I'm convinced that God gives a mother three sons to teach her, for He wants her to learn the power of grace and prayer. For, I surely did.

Love is not an instinct, it is a life commitment. How did I learn this? By the fact that some mothers are selfish and self-centered. They put their needs before those of their children. I'm sure that you have read or seen on T.V. the cases where a mother lets a perverted boyfriend abuse her child physically, mentally and yes, sexually. She knows it is going on, but does nothing about it, fearful he would walk out on her. For whatever reason, none of them are excusable. We parents were the ones given the responsibility to protect our children.

As a pastor's wife, I got to see many dysfunctional families. Our church picked up a lot of children from broken homes, for we had a bus ministry and we saw that they at least went to Sunday school and Worship each week. Many parents were glad just to get rid of them for around three hours each Sunday. Two little boys, in particular, rode the bus. They were over-active, like many little boys are. Since Jim was the pastor, and these boys were a handful for the workers, he would have them sit on the front row with him before he preached. He always put his arm around them, and would whisper how important it was for them to be quiet during the preaching. It worked wonders, though they never were very still. (We ended up with a Children's Church, and that solved the problem.)

Since we tried to visit all the families of the bus kids, we went to their house one evening. The boys were so excited to see us come to visit them. Their step-dad yelled at them for not being still and quiet. It was from sheer joy on their part. Finally, their dad told them to fall out and do twenty push-ups apiece. We could read the fear in their eyes. Mom didn't say a word. We left as quickly as we could for these little boys were just excited. Later, we saw the result of the emotional abuse the mother endured, as it affected her health badly. Some years later, after Jim retired and we went to Mexico, we received a card from a Sunday school teacher. She shared how she taught that God loved them with a perfect, unconditional love. She asked them if anyone had ever loved them that way and if they'd like to make a card and send it to them. One of these little boys said Jim had loved him that way and he made him a card, and she sent it to us. It was a very humbling experience. It taught us that all love is not in vain. We never know what a kind word or action will do to a child, or to an adult, for that matter.

I've observed a mother of a retarded child love and minister to her child year after year. How do they keep on keeping on? They do it by love, commitment, and God's grace. I've seen a mother take care of a grown child, bed-ridden due to a vehicular accident, or another disabled by a thoughtless deed, on a dare. They have no end in sight. How do they do this? They do it by love, commitment, and God's grace. How about an adult child heavily addicted, who comes home time and time again only to get healed and to go off again and his mother dreads each phone call, wondering if he has fallen off the wagon again. Only love, commitment, and God's grace can sustain parents during these times. Parenting can last a long time for some people. We have no guarantees. What do we look forward to? Thanks? No, we look forward to hearing, "Well done, thy good and faithful servant." Look around you, God is teaching you from the negatives.

AS A GRANDMOTHER:

Since my Mom died when I was only eighteen months old and my Dad married when I was four years old, I never knew my birth mother. But I will never forget my introduction to my grandmother I would be living with for years. I was recovering from just having the chicken pox and still had visible scars. The first words I remember her saying was a shocking pronouncement that I looked like death. She kept her distance from me from that moment on. She never hugged me once that I recall. I really don't remember her once saying a loving word to me. She made it quite clear though, to all who visited our home, that I was not a blood grandchild. It was years later that my very loving parents found out how she treated me when they were gone from home.

I had two other grandmothers; my Dad's mother who I was named after, who I loved, but rarely saw, as she lived in Philadelphia. My real Mom's mother who I usually saw once a year, and I loved, and wished she was the one living with us. She died quite young. She lived near her daughter in Swansea, Massachusetts and I never knew much about her family, just that she had only two daughters. I found out years later that she worked and had to put her girls in an orphanage. What I learned from this very negative experience was that when I was a grandmother, I would love my grandchildren and made a commitment to be a good grandmother one day.

I can honestly say I absolutely kept that commitment, despite the fact it took place years later. God blessed us by allowing us to live close to most of our seven grandkids when they were young. We had wonderful times together. We built wonderful memories that neither I nor they will ever forget. We have often taken trips down memory lane to recall those times. When they moved away, they visited often and we visited them.

I will ever wonder how three such imperfect sons could have had such perfect children. I'm sure I over-protected, and over-loved, and doted on them a bit. But I am also the one who prayed the most for them and still do. And I will daily until the day the Lord calls me home.

GREAT GRAND-CHILDREN:

I actually thought I could never love my great, grand-children, as I loved my grand-children. But I can truthfully say that I have been smitten. It is different though, I know they have grandmas and grandpas of their own now. They must increase and we must decrease. Anyhow, we don't have the health, the energy, or the patience that we had when we were young. We could never keep up with them.

Much prayer went up for them before they were born and after. They are very intelligent, healthy, and have good hearts like their parents. I am just as committed, as far as praying for them, as I was for those before them. My family is not all serving the Lord, as I would like them to. But I know God and His desire for them to be all that He and we want them to be. I have placed them in God's care. That is all I can do.

What I Have Learned From My Negatives: Part III

MILITARY WIFE:

One thing I remember about our time in the military is that a wife had to be flexible at all times. Military orders could be expected at any time. Your husband and you had to adjust your lives in accordance to the will of Uncle Sam. We would move to one place and the economy was good, so you lived comfortably. The next military orders sent you to an area where the housing doubled. You had to be an extremely good manager there. When you had to go through a separation, you had expenses for your husband and for you and the family. This was a common experience in those days. So, military life is a constant adjustment.

One of the adjustments was the cultures were different moving in around the U.S.A. If you go from the eastern part of our country to the Deep South, it is like moving to another country. When you did go out of the U.S.A., you found the need to deal with a foreign language. So when you talk about negatives, they were numberless. I certainly learned a few things from these negatives. Marrying a man electing to make a career out of the Air Force was my choice. So my life had to adapt to his choices, or our marriage would never make it.

Most negatives in the military are related to the fact that there were so many separations. Many marriages never could stand Dad being away from the family for extended tours. No one who has never had to deal with this can comprehend what it means to live two different lives for extended periods, and then come home to a totally different situation than you left. For one thing, Mom has been the authority figure for say 1 or 1½ years. Suddenly, Dad is the one who calls the shots. Not to mention how Mom is supposed to feel when she had to do everything alone and now Dad makes the final decisions. Even meal times and slacking a little on rules have changed, but if anything with military men, rules are rules and if you break them, discipline follows.

The deep southern states women were notoriously famous for being Mama's girls. They ran home often. So, often, the marriage ended in divorce. What I learned from that was I didn't have a choice. My husband was a lifer, so was I and the children, also.

I had fervently prayed that Jim and I would never have to go through a long range separation. I didn't care where we went, just so we could go as a family. God answered that prayer, he had to go on a few temporary duty assignments, but we just made that a time to visit family. Another prayer for our Air Force moving was that we would have a good church to go to when we got there. God did this too. We loved our churches. Often, we knew all about our next church before we even moved, from friends who had been members there. Our church family was very dear to us. We became as close to them as we did our own family.

We prayed our children wouldn't be affected by the constant moving. They adapted and it caused them to be extremely out-going. To this day, they have a tremendous sense of direction. Another thing they got from those moving days is that they seemed to never meet a stranger. They could talk to anyone, anywhere. It actually has been a plus for them as they grew into adults. They were just friendly kids. Our youngest son, who moved the least of all, was shy, and he was not as nearly adaptable.

Jim's organization and leadership schools in the Air Force helped him to be a good manager in the churches he pastored. We met many new people and learned to love all kinds of people. Racism is something you never learn in the military, as we met men and women from all nations around the world. All the churches we served in used us in many different areas of service, so we had a wonderful background. Jim walked alongside many godly pastors and he had the best mentoring he could ever get.

All our lives, up until we retired in 1971 from the Air Force, was to prepare us for what God had in store for us as a pastor and pastor's wife. Although we had looked forward to serving in a church in a greater capacity once he was retired, we never dreamed God would call him to the pastorate. We thought we had come to the end of our military era, but found we were simply beginning a new life of service in another branch of fighting soldiers, in the Lord's Army.

What I Have Learned From My Negatives: Part IV

AS A PASTOR'S WIFE:

Ever since I first became a Christian, I theoretically knew of God's greatness and that there was nothing impossible for Him. However, practically, I didn't find out until Jim and I were thrust into the ministry without any formal preparation. Now, after all these years, I know experientially how great our God is, and there is truly nothing impossible with Him. I learned this by jumping into the deep waters and waiting for God's deliverance, time and time again.

There are an abundance of negatives in a church you can learn from. I thank God for placing us in the first church He did, for they were a loving, patient church. They loved us enough to let us make mistakes and profit from them. And they did the same for our three sons. They never expected any more from them than they did from their own children. We have seen so many churches having double standards, what they expect from their children and how they have greater expectations from the pastor's children.

This church was also the one where we spent our pre-retirement years. The church had gone through some hard times during the years we had spent serving in other churches. They had some very good ones too, but had some bad management also.

Many of the people who were there in the beginning were still there, but many had stayed in the two missions we started in the 70's. Many of the miracles we saw in the former years were seen again. I will not cover all the churches God used us in, but here are a few lessons we were taught from the negatives we saw from different churches.

1.   From the great works God did with such incapable people like us, we learned that He is able to do much more than we ever could have expected. Ephesians 3:20-21, (NKJV) says, "Now to Him who is able to do exceedingly abundantly above all that we ask of think, according to the power that works in us, to Him be glory in the church by Christ Jesus to all generations, forever and ever. Amen."

2.   We learned He loves every single person and wants to set them free from their past sins, whether great or small, and save them. He will do that even if we blow it with our big mouths. Jim never knew that there was anyone beyond God's love and forgiveness, for that is what the Bible says. Through our bus ministry and our visits in the homes, we met some pretty shady characters.

One was a motorcycle gang member whose children rode the bus. One asked Jim if he would marry him and his girlfriend. Without thinking twice, he said he would be delighted to. After all, these people were allowing their children to come to Sunday school and church. Jim had prayed for an open door into this group, so what else could he do? The evening of the wedding, we arrived and unbeknownst to us, the whole gang was sitting around an empty room on the floor with one dim light above. A small table was set up for Jim to lay his Bible. The gang leader from our county was the best man. I'll never forget that ceremony as long as I live. If you can imagine coming into that room from our background, you can imagine what I felt like. I still don't know how Jim maintained his composure and joyful spirit through it all. Jim smiled and began the ceremony. He held the Bible in his hand, and spoke of how God created man and placed them in the garden and said it wasn't good that man was alone, so he created a perfect woman for him. He spoke how Jesus placed His seal of approval on this union and said what God had joined together; let not man put asunder, etc.

I had been watching the gang leader, and watched a beautiful transformation take place in his appearance. The hardness began to crack and softness came over him. Afterwards, they asked us to stay for refreshments. Quickly, the gang leader came up and told us it was O.K. He made sure. Jim got a call from this man a couple days later, and he asked Jim if he would marry him and his live-in girlfriend of many years. Jim, of course, was happy they were finally getting married, so he said sure.

Jim shared with our people what God had done, and got a very mixed response. Some thought it was wonderful, some turned up their noses and frowned. Then Jim predicted this man would be saved and his whole family. Not realizing this man's children were there and would go home and repeat his words, it stirred up no small commotion. Jim simply turned it over to God.

Sometime later, a gang from a neighboring big city came and shot up his place. He had someone call from the E.R. at our local hospital and Jim went over to see him. He grabbed Jim's hand and asked him to pray for him. And told him how much he appreciated him coming. To make a long story short, he and his family did come to the Lord and accepted His gift of salvation. They followed with baptism, and their changed life showed the proof of their decision. We definitely found out where the hard hearts in our church were. We learned to never give up hope on any man or woman. And we have never ceased to believe anyone is beyond God's love.

3. We found many people use their talents and gifts for self-promotion. Any pastor has had to watch great performances. But, that

just teaches us we have to pray for them a lot, so they will give these talents and gifts to the Lord and will grow up in Him.

4.   There is always, in any church, people who love the church building and they spend much time seeing that it is always perfect. Of course, they get very nervous when a busload of snotty-nosed children, with their dirty hands and shoes, arrive. Jim and I learned people are way more important than buildings. Many churches today will die when their gray haired members die, for there are no youth or children at all. And they wonder why. With all the garbage dumped on our young minds today, if we don't reach them when they are young, they may never give their hearts to God. We had better wake up, and learn from these negative teachings.

5.   Also, we saw in some churches that some charter members think that because they were there in the beginning of the work, they owned the church. They have been instruments of the devil for years. I nearly dropped when one Sunday Jim announced from the pulpit that as of tomorrow morning, Monday, he would kick down every door in this church that is locked. This is God's house, and we will use it all. One chartered member had a huge ring with keys to every closet in the church. Our custodians couldn't even get a roll of toilet paper without going through him. The following morning, all doors were unlocked. He had a giant printer from which he did all the church's printing. There is no telling how long he held up people waiting for his convenience. Jim and our secretary solved that problem; they pitched in and bought a new office printer, and one by one, his ownership was taken away from him.

What did we learn? God is in control, not man, if you will just yield the church to Him. All you need is a Word from God. That is sufficient. When we left the church, which had been in great debt, they had a plant worth over a million dollars debt free. And this was in the early 80's when a million dollars was a lot of money. Our God is able.

6.   Mostly, despite Jim's harshness at times, he was mostly loved and appreciated. A few spread lies trying to intimidate him. He always believed

vengeance was the Lord's, as God says in His Word. He never would stoop to other's tactics. He learned a clear conscience was better than having the last word. Lies cannot stand the test of time, and never have.

In all the years that I was a pastor's wife, God drew me closer to Him. Oh, we ran into countless negatives, but each and every one brought us to a new knowledge of Him and His amazing grace. If only young pastors could walk alongside a seasoned pastor for several years, they could learn much about the Lord from their experiences. May He get all the glory?

When To and When Not to Help?

In all the churches we have either been members of, or Jim has pastored, there have been those who needed financial help. If you are fortunate enough to have people in your church to form a committee to handle these affairs, you are blessed, indeed. We have been a part of large and small churches, so we have seen both.

Some have had a working committee made up of people who were capable of good financial management, and had the wisdom to detect and decide if those asking for help would need their assistance, had a genuine need, or if the church would be helping them or hindering them. You see at times, a person's lack was simply due to mismanagement. If our church were to continue to help bail them out, they would only be enabling them to waste their money.

We are definitely, as a church body, to be alert to and tend to the emergencies that can and do crop up. However, there should be money set aside for this. It would be better to err in meeting a false need, than in missing a genuine need.

After you have gotten a family out of trouble and they continue to have the same need over and over again, there is a deep rooted problem. Most, but not all times, there is a management problem. Money is spent on non-essentials and when faced with rent, utilities, food, or car expenses, they run out of money and cry for help.

This is where a capable benevolence, or finance committee, comes in handy. They can, through talking about this matter with them, detect the cause of their problem. A pastor is not the best person to handle this or a person who can't say "No," even if saying no would be best. It takes much prayer and wisdom to handle these situations.

Some churches use their deacons if the church is small. This can work out, unless they have been chosen for their servant spirit and are also too tender-hearted to check the need out before giving. Christians ought to be convicted about their finances. It is a very bad testimony for a Christian not to pay their bills. God knows their needs. He cares about their needs, and perhaps He is teaching them to trust Him more. Why? Perhaps, He is trying to work it out where they will change their ways and be a good steward. After all, it is all the Lord's money.

It is also such a great testimony when you are depending upon Him and He comes through supernaturally. It is also a great testimony when a loving God stretches our income to go far beyond our own means. Two people can live next door to each other, one with a large income and one with a minimum one. Yet, they live the same lifestyle. How? It could be that God is blessing, or it could be that one is mismanaging and the other is managing their money.

After Jim retired from being a pastor, we lived in Mexico for eleven years. We went down to do voluntary missions and also enjoy the sunshine and sea. Jim preached in an American community church, as there were quite a few retired Americans there. I went into the villages, taught literacy, ESL, and taught Mexican women how to plan, prepare, and teach

Children's Sunday school lessons and bringing some materials. Since I did this mainly in homes, I got a good chance to see how they lived.

Americans do not know what poverty is, believe me. Most Mexican families live in a tar paper shack, with dirt floors, and are lucky if they have a table and couple of chairs. They have a hole in the ground outside for a bathroom, cook outside on a wood fire, and have no refrigerator and only a few clothes. Yet, they are always happy. If a man can find work, he spends it for flour, beans, and cornmeal, so he can feed his family. If he is lucky, he runs an electric extension cord to the one family member who has electricity, and he will share it with them. Children? Oh, however many they have, they are blessings of God. And the children are happy, too.

My grandchildren, like so many others, are spoiled. They came to visit us and soon realized the meaning of the true value of things. Their priorities changed, realizing how blessed they were to live in the U.S.A. I feel that this was one of the best teaching experiences they had in those eleven years. I'm proud that above all else they care for people less blessed than they were. They all have giving hearts. But they have also learned some of what people call "needs are merely wants". Some folk look at others and want more, and more and more. Yet, somehow they cannot separate themselves from the fact that to some, God gives much and to others, less. Many times, it is for their good. The key is can you be like Paul, content in whatever state you are in? Philippians 4:11, (NKJV) says, "Not that I speak in regard to need, for I have learned in whatever state I am, to be content." Oh, what a gift is the joy of contentment.

Gratitude for what we have is disappearing. I believe it would do our youth a great benefit if they went to visit a 3rd world country, and look at what little others have and yet are happy. It might change their outlook and goals for the future.

Up until, now I have not mentioned tithing. I know many think that was only for the Old Testament times when they were under the Law, and now we are in the age of Grace. I believe that also. But, we still tithe, not because of law, but because of love. I have never believed any of what I own is mine. It is all of God. Somehow, God led us to give Him 10% or more. And blessings, we didn't give to get, but oh how our Lord has supernaturally blessed us. I cannot explain it, other than "God". If anyone has never tried this, he should. It works!

Where Are Our Youth?

One of the greatest reasons that youth abandon God's plan for their life in their teenage years is their uncontrolled sexual desires. In God's infinite wisdom, He left some holy no's and some guidelines for sex and for marriage. One of the admonitions is found in 2 Timothy 2:22, (NKJV), which says, "Flee also youthful lusts; but pursue righteousness, faith, love, peace with those who call on the Lord out of a pure heart." All too often, during teenage years, we are ignorant of the reason for these guidelines. Many base their choices on feelings. And feelings can be deceptive.

It actually astounds me how many young people have abandoned the command that they remain pure for their mate God has selected for them. It isn't even a consideration in the society we live in. And many of God's children feel they can participate in sex outside of marriage, without consequences, because everyone is doing it and everyone seems to have accepted it. Even those professed Christians do it and think it is O.K.

Another reason is the church avoids touching on this very delicate matter. Why? In the 1980's through the year 2000, many churches would not deal with it, fearing they would lose their youth. And how did that work for us? Where are all our youth today? A boat can become weak from a tiny crack in the hull, if not fixed. These tiny cracks of compromise have shipwrecked the faith of our youth.

One reason the Lord has told us not to participate in sex outside of marriage is because of the great love He has for us. He doesn't want us to have to experience the tragic consequences that come with breaking this law of His. If a young woman finds out she is pregnant from even a single sexual encounter, her life is changed forever. She has many choices according to the world: abortion, go to a relative in a different state, give up the child for adoption, let her parents raise the child, a shot gun marriage, or raise the child herself and forfeit her plans for the future. The latter is the ONLY real option for a Christian.

What about the young man? He might end up giving up a sports scholarship, or one for scholastic achievement, to work to support a child he was in no way prepared to have, but feels he must accept his duty. This is not a basis to start a life upon, as it will affect him the rest of his life.

What about repentance on the part of both parties, and getting married and making a home for the child. Yes, this happens, and can work with committed parents and the couple. But it is not easy, and definitely will not be without hard knocks.

Most youth have not grown spiritually enough to make the right choice if they're guided by feelings alone. We cannot blame the government, the schools, or even the churches when this happens. The responsibility has been laid upon our shoulders, we are the parents. Since being in retirement, I cannot tell you how many times we have seen grandparents raising their children's children. They didn't think it could ever happen to them, and now when they should be in retirement, they are trying to make up for some of theirs and their children's mistakes.

Have you been a good example to your children? Or, have you been guilty of "cafeteria style" religion yourself? You know, you take out of religion what you want, and you leave the rest. Have you had open, honest communications with your children about the blessings of obedience, and the consequences of disobedience? At times, we are so caught up in our own "time pressure existence" we leave others to do the job He gave to us.

We are the ones God placed this responsibility upon. Speak about accountability. If we have never held our children accountable for their actions, do not be surprised if all the above comes knocking at your door.

There are other reasons youth are not attending church today, but this so-called sexual revolution is definitely a major cause. Teach your children well parents, or you may find yourself getting another chance, teaching your grandchildren. This time, you will with much prayer.

Your teens may tell you they have a right to choose any sex they prefer in a marriage partner. Be sure to make a stand and read Mark 10:6-8, (NKJV), which states, "From the beginning of the creation, God made them male and female. For this reason a man shall leave his father and mother and be joined to his wife, and the two shall become one flesh, so then they are no longer two, but one flesh."

Marriage between a man and a woman has been here since time began. Why is it, suddenly, what has been called perversion for ages, some are calling a matter of choice? My Dad was not a Christian for many years of his life. But let me tell you if you told him this was right, he would have had a heart attack. This may not be politically correct, but it is Biblically so.

Whether To, or Not To?

Tithing will not save anyone. Let's get that straight up front. We as Christians are not under Law, but Grace. Yet, we must understand that Jesus did not come to destroy the Law, but to fulfill it. (Matthew 5:17) Rather than do away with it, Jesus went deeper. He wants us to follow the spirit of the Law, not the letter of the Law. There is a vast difference in that.

To me, tithing is one of the disciplines of the Christian life. Keeping this Old Testament command doesn't lead to salvation, only Christ can save us by His grace, through faith. (Romans 5:1-2, 10:9-10, NKJV) But by keeping them, there is great reward. The closer we follow God's standards, the more we are blessed. Many a child of God never gets in on God's best, because he never reads, digests, and applies the Word to his or her life.

Now, I am not saying that keeping God's moral, spiritual standards will automatically free one of all adversity in life, because that just isn't guaranteed. We've already stressed that God often uses this in the process of spiritual maturity. But, the very best place to be to experience the fruit of being God's child is to be in the center of God's will.

I have experienced, and am presently experiencing, much adversity, but I am learning God's grace is truly amazing and sufficient. I can have peace, because I know all is well between my God and me.

When it comes to the question of should I, as a Christian, tithe or not, read why I and others do. (Malachi 3:8-12) I am simply taking God at His Word. I prove I love Him by my actions, which back up or support my words. I also trust what God says to be true. I have tested and proved His Word is true, over and over again. I no longer have to continue to do so. I want to remain in the spiritual position where I can be blessed. I just cannot out give God. The more I give, the more He puts in.

I know God loves all His children equally, but I cannot doubt His Word in this matter. In the secular, very materialistic society we live in, not to give to the church Christ died for is to me pure selfishness. We do not withhold spending money on our every whim, why can't we give God that very small percentage of the money He has blessed us with? No other nation on earth has been blessed by God as this one has. I have travelled much in my life and have always been amazed at this phenomenon. Let us never forget where these blessings have come from. There is a song "Give Of Your Best To The Master".[6] Our lives should be a visible demonstration of this practice to the world around us. Even Muslims give up their lives for Allah, a false God. Shouldn't we as followers of the one true God be as dedicated?

I have been mocked by my giving practices. Some have told me the Old Testament is not practical or to be heeded today. Yet, when I look at Jim's and my life, and how God has supernaturally provided for each and every need more than I ever asked for, I am convinced it is right for me and I will give the tithe, no matter what. I have tested God, and His Word is true, from the cover to the maps.

---

[6] Grose, Howard B. (1902) and Barnard, Charlotte A. (1864) "Give of Your Best to the Master".

Worship

Genuine worship begins in our hearts. It can happen in a worship service, as God does meet with His people in a special way, when they come together in a special place to meet Him. But, if you have the most awesome church in town, the best choir around with lots of great music, an eloquent preacher, and your church is famous for such that is no guarantee God will show up and touch your heart.

Sometimes, the best worship I've had, and I'm sure I'm not the only one, was when I was alone in my secret place where I meet with God. Mine is in my living room next to the fireplace. This is where I have had the sweetest fellowship with God. Why do some people enjoy the church worship service, but hardly get from the pew to the car before they have totally forgotten the whole service?

Once, when my youngest son moved to Virginia, he had to seek a new church home. We couldn't wait until he would e-mail us in Mexico, where we were living at the time. This was the way we communicated. We had told him to e-mail us as soon after church as he could, and tell us all what it was like. We got an e-mail soon after his church was over. There were only two words in it. "SHOW TIME!" We know our crazy son so well and we didn't have to guess what he was telling us. Going to church was like going to a play with a great performance. But it definitely was not worship. The Holy Spirit, the Power Source, never showed up. How sad!

But getting back to true worship, we have a responsibility to prepare to receive it. The best way is to pray for the service before we even leave home. Pray for your pastor, the music, and that decisions will be made for Christ that day. You must expect to be blessed when you go to meet the Lord. If you start with a negative attitude, you will probably have a negative experience, and leave with a negative attitude, finding fault with everything and everyone.

Expect to meet God. Don't look at the title of the message and say, "Oh, I'm glad Jane is here, she sure needs this." Start with the question, "What has God to say to me today?" Examine yourself, confess any known sin. Eliminate from your mind any distractions, such as dinner, kids, friends, schedules, etc. Now, your heart is ready. Simply wait for the Lord to speak to you. Isaiah 55:6, (NKJV) says, "Seek the Lord while he may be found; call upon him while he is near." He wants to speak to you more than you want to speak to Him. Experiencing a worship experience is a wonderful thing. And I believe you can if you are in the right frame of mind and heart, even though the pastor and others that lead worship are not what they ought to be.

I have gone to churches, as I am sure you have, that the people who lead are in the flesh, and have wanted to leave. But when I would ask the Lord about leaving, He would tell me I needed to teach and mirror with my life what God wanted to change. That is the real reason God sent me to this church. As fleshly actions are caught, so are righteous attitudes. Let God use you to change the worship service by your right actions. And don't forget the power that is yours in prayer. God can change hearts, and you may be the catalyst He will use to do it where He has placed you.

Need of Many Today

Have you ever thought about just how many people today work at the countless jobs that require them to work shift work? Now, I know, some of them do it by choice. But, I have seen with my own eyes many who do not have a choice. Among them are first responders, doctors, nurses, firemen, cops, military men and women, nursing home workers, retail, or service workers. Even some in maintenance work at airports. At some plants, days off go by seniority and they may wait years for someone to retire, so they will get a chance to work normal hours, and get weekends off.

Now, I've heard the cliché about, "If you are offered a job and it involves shift work, just don't take it." "Wait for a better one." Or, "You can still go to Sunday evening service." Unfortunately, many churches today do not have a Sunday evening service. First of all, consider this. Some have pressing family and financial needs. They may have been laid off in this world's economy, due to cutbacks. If you get behind, it is hard to catch up. Not all men can afford to pass up a good paying job, because of shift work. You might be able to go to Wednesday prayer meeting, but this usually is not worship. Also today, if we are lucky, we are likely to have a very small group, with a short, not meaty Bible Study, allowing time for prayer.

Satan loves to get a person cut off from one's Sunday morning re-charging at Worship Service in our churches. It's the same as the old coyote who looks for that one steer who gets cut off from the herd. They are vulnerable. So it is with a person who has been cut off from his or her Power Source. Like a steer, they are weak and more vulnerable the farther they stray. The longer they stay gone, the easier they are to prey upon.

Wouldn't it be wonderful if there was another evening when these shift workers could go to a worship service other than Sunday morning worship? When then? A meeting would have to be called to see when would be the best time for your church. What about the poor pastor you say? He could simply preach the same message as he did Sunday, and music could be the same.

Another problem solved would be if another person missed the Sunday service, they also could attend later. The Catholic Church has Saturday evening services. Many attend in place of Sunday. I am not advocating the need to make Sunday available for more play time. I just wonder if we couldn't provide a way to meet this very important need.

Another need I have observed that isn't being met by most churches is the making disciples of the recently saved and people who have not been trained in the Word of God. One often wonders if the reason a person comes to the Lord, but soon drops out of sight is because he wasn't truly saved. Or is it because we older Christians fail to get alongside of him and check on him immediately when he is absent. If he has a need, we need to see that need is met. After all, it is not a lost person's normal habit to go to church weekly. It is easy to go back to the old habits. Sometimes, he needs encouragement to avail himself of the things that will help him grow. That is why a New Member's class is so beneficial. Among other things, it will show a new convert the importance of attending church meetings. It is not just tradition.

One of Satan's tactics is like what an old rancher told me once. He said he watched how coyotes worked. They hung around the herd, and when one got away from the protection of the herd, he would attack. Not only did he get those who were cut off from the herd, but they waited around a pregnant cow, and as soon as she gave birth, the coyote would eat the newborn calf. Satan is real. We must realize once he has lost a person's soul to salvation, the next best thing is to keep that person from growing and being used by God. What better way than to keep him from going to church.

A church has to meet needs, all needs. Sometimes, we are so caught up with what a church can do for us, and our family, that we fail to see the needs of others that are not being met. Jesus went out of His way to meet the need of one person. If we are to do the same, we have to evaluate who we are not meeting the needs of. There are others as well as these two needs, like the home-bound, and nursing home residents, as well. This certainly varies from place to place. Our churches are really spiritual hospitals to heal broken hearts, broken lives, and broken families. Is ours?

You Are Already Retired

Much has been said about when you should retire. What is the best age to start talking about health issues, etc? Some people don't retire when they should, for one reason or another. I think you can answer the question, when should I retire? One question you could ask yourself is when can I tell that I am ready?

Is retirement a topic of my conversation often? Do I long for the day I can retire? Do I have to make myself go to work? Do I dread the work I once loved? Do I have to act a lot at work to make it look like I really enjoy what I do, but I don't anymore? Do I speak negatively of the job to others? If you answer yes to the above, you have reached the age you should retire. For you are most likely retired already.

Actually, money is the only reason you don't retire right now. You just don't see how you can make it on a retirement income. Not only do you speak of it a lot, but it shows in your work. You know, you make more and more excuses to take time off. You go on vacation often, and even do it if you have to use your family as an excuse; you do it as often as you can. Like a backslider, little by little, you stray from your job. Others see your lack of preparation, and can tell your heart is no longer in your work. You have a divided mind and it is obvious.

In reality, you would do yourself a great favor if you were to retire right now, not only to you, but to others as well. Really, you are already retired. Your mate probably has already figured you out. Mates are like that. They study us and figure us out a long time before we admit what is really going on in our minds and actions. If by some chance you are a pastor, or staff member, your church has perhaps been aware of your feelings for a long time. You see, whether you know it or not, it has already affected your preaching and leadership.

The biggest problem with preachers is if it is God's perfect will for you to retire, He could just be changing directions in your life. He wants you to retire, as He has something else planned for you. I can testify that though my husband retired from being a pastor in 1995, he certainly didn't quit ministering. The Lord sent us to Mexico for eleven years where we did volunteer mission work. When he came home when God told us he had other plans for us, Jim filled the pulpit whenever and wherever God opened a door. It is so interesting to see how God used us in so many different areas after we retired.

The first of October of 2015, Jim preached his last sermon due to severe back pain. He was 82 years old, and even then, it was hard for him to quit. Not for the money, for a lot of times when churches were struggling, he insisted on them not paying him.

The strangest thing of all is how we lived on such a small income in retirement, yet, we never lacked a thing. Truly God can stretch the smallest income, and you will live as well as someone who makes twice as much, or more than you do. If only people could catch this fact. If God is in your retiring, He will meet all your needs and then some. I cannot explain it, but it is so, and I can testify of that truth by our lives.

The only concern of any Christian is what does God want? Do not look at anything else but that. If it is His will, He will take care of your needs. This is simply a new area of trust for you. God doesn't change just because you are retiring. He is love, and He is faithful, and His promise in Jeremiah 32:27, (NKJV) pertains to retirement too.

In retirement, my husband and I both had cancer, and are survivors. I have had two hip replacements, a knee replacement, two hand and one foot surgery. The great news is that it hasn't slowed me down much, though in a month, I will be 78 years old. My good health comes from the Lord, and He wants me to continue ministering to Jim and teaching a Ladies Sunday school class. When God is finished with Jim and I, He will take us home, and what a wonderful day that will be. My kids, grandkids, and great grandkids will be fine, for they will be in God's hands. There is no better place to be. That is all they need.

You Simply Need an Honest, Open Heart

It can be put many ways, but as simply put as I know, (many have chosen better words than I) Christianity is much more than religion, it is a relationship. It is more than a ritual, it is being, and acting as a child of God. If you ask a person if they are a Christian, many will tell you they are Catholic, Lutheran, Presbyterian, Mormon, Muslim, etc. But their lives bear fruit of a black heart. The nature of a true Christian is that of Christ and he or she has a heart for truth. Whoever he or she is matters not. John 3:16, (KJV) and the song written by Philip Bliss say it all. "Whosoever Will May Come."[7]

If a person has a heart for truth, that person will find it. I can testify I had a heart for truth and was never satisfied till I found it. And when I did find it, I knew it was the truth. You see, I was steeped in Catholicism, rules, rituals, and regulations of the church. Unfortunately, this isn't Christianity. Oh, I know we should know what we believe, but it is so much more to know WHOM we believe in and then do something about it. Accept that we were born in sin so we are sinners, we could never earn or buy

---

[7] Bliss, P.P. "Whosoever Will May Come". Written during the winter of 1869-70 after hearing Mr. H. Moorhouse (from England) preach on St. John iii. 16.

salvation, but we could accept what God provided for us. Payment for the penalty of sin, on an old cruel cross so that if we believe it with all our heart, we will receive the gift of salvation. Jesus said He was the only way, (there is no other way) the only truth, and the only life. (Eternal, unending) no man one comes to the Father except through me. (John 14:6, NKJV)

Then, because of that great love that provided us with eternal life, and all the blessings of such a life, we want to love and serve Him from our heart. How can I stress the importance of getting it out of our head, and into our heart? Head belief will not do it, it involves a commitment that comes from the heart, and heart faith changes a life to be what God wants us to be, not what we think we should, or others think we ought to be.

Many never find truth, though they will tell you they have long sought it. The reason they never found it was that God knew they had no disposition for obedience. (The willing acceptance of Jesus' rules in their life.) Before they were born, God simply knew they lacked an honest open heart, and always would. It is a short distance from the head to the heart, but it makes all the difference in the world. He loves us so much that He will take great means to move it. How long that takes is up to you.

Seasons of Life

As we look outdoors, we can clearly see the changing of the seasons. When spring arrives, we see the crocus break through the ground, tulips popping their heads in the flower bed, trees in all their glory blooming, and soon many growing plants. Everything seems new and beautiful. It reminds us of when we were first married. It seems like we just started a new life. Those were such happy days. Soon, our homes were filled with laughter, new babies had arrived, and there was the patter of little feet running, filled with laughter. Those were the days of wonder and new beginnings. It was hard many times to think those days could ever end. How we rejoiced in them.

Then came the Summertime. Summer brought its own sources of joy. We basked in the warmth of the days. It was true we would have some hot uncomfortable days, but we didn't think of them. We were too busy enjoying the full grown gardens, flowers, and vegetables flourishing. The smell of blossoms and cut grass was so welcoming. The children were thriving, growing like weeds, and enjoying all the outings that come with summer days. There were baseball games, swimming at the lake, canoeing, sleepovers, and camping in tents. Oh, if these days could continue forever.

Then came Fall. I have to admit that Fall is my very favorite time of the year. I look forward to it coming, especially after a long hot summer. It is when we reap harvests. We live in ranch country, so it is not unusual to see hay cutting, baling, or boys bucking hay, which is simply loading it on trailers or trucks. It's wonderful to go to the farm markets and get the fresh vegetables. I learned to can and freeze many that we grew ourselves. And since we live where there are many fruit trees, we learned to make jams and jellies, as well. It was so good to look forward to the blessings we would have in the Winter.

Another harvest we enjoyed is seeing our children finish their schooling and reap the harvest of the years they spent studying to get that first job. Now, they had it and were looking back thinking all that homework was worth all the hours spent doing it. We were looking forward to retirement and were finally becoming financially fit. We often thought of what we would do when retirement came. Of course, we were looking forward to that. Children married their sweethearts; the precious grandchildren came along, and of course after that, didn't think it could get any better.

Then came Winter. Oh, it is so cold in winter in Colorado. Of course that means skiing, and other winter sports, but it is amazing how cold one gets when they get older. It seems I was always cold. That was solved when Jim retired and said we would head south of the border. We had gone to Mexico many times on vacation and thought about retiring there. So, we ended up selling our house and everything but a few things in it and headed there. We did missions, but we also enjoyed the pleasant weather and the bay we lived on.

All too often, Winter is drab. There is the beauty of snow, but it either gets dirty, or it just disappears in warmer areas. It is so wonderful to look up to the mountains and see they are snow-capped and beautiful. I guess it is how you look at the seasons. Activities seem to dwindle, days are shorter, and the cold makes you want to stay indoors. Many cannot move to Alaska for this reason. The summers sound fabulous with the long days, but the winters are just too confining and drab.

As I think about the four seasons in a year, I realize there is another way to look at them. That is to compare them to our spiritual lives. Unfortunately, I did not come to the Lord until I was leaving my teens.

How I wish I could've learned the Bible when I was a child. But, one cannot look at what could've, should've, or would've been. So, I was a new born babe in Christ when I was eighteen years old. That was my Spring. When I found salvation, I was truly the happiest person alive. I wanted everyone to know what I knew, and to have what I had. I certainly didn't have much Bible knowledge, but I hungered and thirsted for the things of the Lord.

My Summer was when many older, more mature Christians helped me to learn more and were wonderful tutors. I needed love, and they showed it to me. I was weak, and didn't have many convictions, but they showed me the way. I cannot emphasize enough how other Christians helped me to grow during that time. My husband was in the Air Force then, and he also grew much during that time. Little did anyone know what the Lord had in store for us, but they helped us prepare for that time. God reaped the harvest that they had sown during those years.

Fall to me was that time when Jim realized he couldn't keep up all the work of a pastor and thought about retirement. I also saw Jim begin to wither. I honestly was not surprised. Because he was retiring from being pastor in no way meant that his service in the ministry was over. It was just that beautiful time when age takes over, and we get ready for the real retirement that is in store for all of us. Retirement was definitely not dreary or drab to us. It was definitely different. God had reaped a harvest of souls in Jim's years as pastor, now we were in a strange country, they spoke a different language, their culture was different, but they needed Jesus.

We saw many souls won for the Lord, both American and Mexican during those eleven years. We built a home, and yes, the fishing was great. We had a Bible study in our home and took the best of both worlds. Those were wonderful, productive years seeing all the possibilities God would work out through those we ministered to. We left Mexico, because at that time, the Mexican Christians were thriving and able to do the work themselves. We did not want them to rely on us to do what they could do for themselves.

Winter was for us coming home and buying a new house. We were beginning to feel our age. We had lots of snow on the mountains, (our hair). Isaiah 46:4, (NKJV) says, "Even to your old age, I am He, and even to gray hairs I will carry you!" And we were beginning to feel our age more as the years passed. The Lord led us to go to one of the missions our church started when Jim was pastor. I was given the opportunity to teach a Ladies Sunday school class, which I absolutely loved. Jim filled the pulpit for pastors out of their churches. Time was creeping up on us. We sold our house of eleven years and downsized to one we could keep up. (Three doors from the last one.) Then Jim got sick. Our bodies were no longer firm and strong. We could tell we were not what we used to be. Our activities definitely slowed down. By then, both of us were cold all the time. We went from having seven grandchildren, to having eight great, grandchildren who we loved as much as all the others.

Jim passed from this life, to eternal life at the ripe old age of 82. He lacked a month of being 83. Winter is gone now, and Spring is showing signs of coming anew. The cycle of life is ever marching on. We enjoy each and every season as they come, no matter what age we are with the Lord.

Grace, Grace, Marvelous Grace!

There are words that have multiple meanings. One such word is *grace*. Most of us were taught that grace is unmerited favor. (Not earned or deserved.) But few people realize how many forms of grace are given to a child of God.

There is, of course, *saving grace* of which most are familiar with. This grace is found in (Ephesians 2:8-9, KJV), "For by grace are you saved by faith, and that not of yourself, it is a gift f God." There is living, or *sustaining grace*, (2 Corinthians 12:7-9, NKJV) the ability to live under whatever circumstances life has dealt to you. "And lest I should be exalted above measure by the abundance of the revelations, a thorn in the flesh was given to me, a messenger of Satan to buffet me, lest I be exalted above measure. Concerning this thing I pleaded with the Lord three times that it might depart from me. And He said to me, 'My grace is sufficient for you, for My strength is made perfect in weakness.'" (Though, it is sometimes the result of our bad choices.)

There is *dying grace*. This is grace that is given to you solely for the purpose of dying. We do not ever get it until the time we need it. So naturally, we do not understand it, because until we experience it, we cannot know what it is. But all God's grace is sufficient for all manner of life's experiences.

Thank God, I have experienced all of the types of grace mentioned above. The reason I thank God is that I knew about saving grace and sustaining grace, but I didn't know what dying grace was. Oh I had heard about it, but had a very deep fear of the dying part. I didn't fear where I was going for I definitely had a firm security as a Believer. You see, as a pastor's wife, I had seen different people die, gasping for that last bit of oxygen they could get. And I have to admit that I never liked pain.

In December of 1999, after being brought back to my room from thyroid cancer surgery, I coded. It all happened so fast I certainly didn't have time to do anything except know I was dying. I said under my breath, "Well, Lord, looks like I'm coming home early." Suddenly, the most awesome peace came over me. I had never experienced this before, nor have I ever since I was resuscitated. I have given testimony of this experience to fellow children of God, and they theoretically agree it happened, but they don't really know what I am talking about. Many have asked me if I saw a great light, or if I had an out-of-body experience. No, I did not. They must, however, know that *dying grace* is there when they need it.

"I can do all things through Christ who strengthens me." (Philippians 4:13, NKJV), that is what grace is. I saw my 54 year old son die of a brain tumor. He was a perfect specimen of a man, physically, mentally, and emotionally. No son could ever be born that brought more joy to his parents. How did he die? He died well! He prepared me, his mom, and his dad, and everyone he loved, for the coming certainty. He had a type of brain tumor, a geoblastoma that left him with no more than four months to live, no matter what he did. He gave glory to God to the very end. He told fellow law enforcement members who he'd known for years, he was dying for them, so they would come to the Lord, and he hoped he wasn't dying in vain.

No one could do this, in their own strength. He taught many Christians how, too, they should die. He gave glory to the end and told friends and family to be ready for we never know when we will receive the news he had. It was *dying grace*.

In all these years, I have come to the realization that my greatest fears were unfounded. If I was ever to be kidnapped, or one of my children, grandchildren, or great grandchildren would be, this would be my greatest horror. Could I get through something like that? There is only one way. GRACE. And as hard as it would be, we should prepare our children to call upon God for GRACE. If David, Joseph, and Daniel could live in captivity, away from family support, and yet become great men of God, then God's grace is sufficient.

This is the kind of faith we need. And though most of us have never experienced this type of grace, it is something we need to know about and put our trust in the One who has promised to give all we need when we need it. Believe me it is real, and God will give it to you when you need it.

When my husband died in February of 2016, I got a new dose of grace. It is one thing to know practically about grace, but when you see a mate die, you have to call on God for grace every day. Especially if your spouse has done all the bills, banking, trash, outdoor chores, and much more, and you hate to deal with the phone. I had to call on the Lord often, and I can testify as I am still doing this, His grace is sufficient. I can testify of this. I have actually thought a few times that something must be wrong with me. I was married so many years, yet I don't feel the grief that others have shared with me of their experience at the time they lost a mate. I loved Jim dearly, and he loved me. Since he has been really retired, we have spent most every night and day together. Surely, I should miss Jim more than I do.

Why is it we do that? Don't I know the only reason is due to God pouring out His grace for me? I am so busy, it helps. I have so much to be grateful for. Family, friends, and neighbors have stepped in and met so many of my needs. The love that has been poured out upon me is almost unreal. Why am I surprised? Isn't this just exactly what He promised He would do? Why am I awed? All I can say is that I now have an understanding of what God meant when He said He was the I AM. He is everything I need Him to be. When Jesus said I AM the bread of life, the Light of the world, the Good Shepherd, the Vine, wasn't He telling me that whatever I needed was Who He Was and what He would do for me. Like God, He is the exact image of God and will meet whatever need I have. This is GRACE.

Now I have an experiential knowledge of God's Amazing Grace.

Sufficient

If there is one word I could use that would summarize what God is to me, it would be SUFFICIENT. I don't care what need I have, or have ever had, physically, emotionally, or spiritually, God has met that need.

Like so many people, my needs have been many and varied throughout the years. Some have been great, and though some seemed quite insignificant to me, at the time, they were huge. One thing I have learned, whether great or small, they were equal in God's eyes. None of my needs, or those of others, are beyond His ability.

A good illustration I heard that best described this was the following. A man had finally bought his dream car, a Rolls Royce. He was enthralled with the car, as it had exceeded all his highest hopes. He wondered how much power it had, as he feared driving it too fast to check it out. So, he wrote the company and asked just how much power this car possessed. He waited and waited for an answer, but none came. Then, he wrote again and asked the same question. Still, he received no answer. Finally, he couldn't bear it any longer, and wrote the company this question. "Just how much power does this car have, I want to know." A short while later, he received a letter from the company, with one word on it: "SUFFICIENT."

Doesn't this say it all? This car had all the power it needed to have, and then some. No one could ever use all it had. Our God is like that. If He could cause the blind to see, heal the lame from birth, cast out demonic spirits, turn rocks into bread, water into the best wine, change a man from a hopeless alcoholic, or a drug addict into a wonderful husband, godly father, good worker, a blessing to society, or even a preacher or missionary, now that is Unlimited Power!

We have read the many miracles God did in the Old Testament giving us a progressive revelation into the character of our Holy God. Then, when Jesus Christ came into the world, we saw the supreme revelation of God the Father through His Son. Why is it when we are confronted with a need, we fail to remember all we have learned about God's unlimited love and His promises to answer all our prayers, and meet our every need.

All we need to do is line up our lives with His perfect will, so He can be a vehicle of His Omnipotence. (His Almighty, unlimited power.) Every week, as I go to teach my Sunday school lesson, I feel so humbled by the fact I am so ill-equipped. But the wonder of it all is to see my prayers filled through the teaching. You see, I always ask Him to teach the lesson and let me be merely a microphone for Him to speak through.

I had never questioned God's power until Jim was diagnosed with cancer, after having been treated for pain for months and though we still prayed and prayed, no answer came. Then after a visit to Mayo Clinic, they and other doctors found they had treated symptoms, but in actuality, he had had Multiple Myeloma for a long time. (A form of cancer)That is what had been causing the pain. After some time in the hospital with no relief from side effects of chemotherapy, and seeing him suffer, I pled with the Lord for an answer. Why was He not healing Jim, who had been such a faithful servant?

That night, God simply spoke to me, and reminded me He could heal Jim in a minute. But, His ways were not my ways and past my understanding. His mighty power was the same, He hadn't changed. But His will was not my will. I cried much, for I knew that theoretically. The next day, when I visited Jim at the hospital, Jim also had talked with God. He told me He was going home. He didn't mean to our house. He meant to his heavenly home. It was time. He died as soon as our family came home and I am forever reminded that just because God doesn't use His power, isn't because He has less than He always had. It just isn't what He is doing.

At the funeral, I saw so many people who reminded me of how Jim could and did follow God's will, and because of it, they were saved. And some said their whole family was saved today, because Jim preached the whole counsel of God. That is power!

Jim died February13, 2016.

Death Explained

Occasionally in life, death takes one by surprise. Oh, we know it can and will happen to all of us, but we are never prepared when the time comes. We even know the verses that clearly speak to us about death. Ecclesiastes 3:1-2a, (NKJV) tells us, there is a time to be born and a time to die. "To everything there is a season, a time for every purpose under heaven: A time to be born, and a time to die;" Ecclesiastes 7:2, (NKJV) tells us: "Better to go to the house of mourning than to go to the house of feasting. For that is the end of all men; and the living will take it to heart." It is the destiny of every man; the living should take this to heart.

There have been times, when a person's death was expected, either due to old age, chronic sickness, or after a long illness. Though, they will be missed, we rejoice for if they belong to Christ, they have fulfilled God's plan for their lives and have entered into eternal joy. Psalms 116:15 says, "Precious in the sight of the Lord is the death of His saints." We have the assurance in that our loved one has simply left this old worn out body, and gone home to be with the Lord. That is marvelous. Frankly, we will be glad to get rid of this old sinful, sick, weary body when that day comes. Paul even said, "For me to live is Christ, and to die is gain." (Philippians 1:21, NKJV)

The times we have problems is when death comes to a person, whether a family member or a godly man whose life really counts for Christ. We reason that it doesn't make sense to us, for he was so needed for the cause of Christ. A good example of this to me was when Pastor Adrian Rogers of Memphis, Tennessee and Pastor James Kennedy of Florida died. Their televised services reached so many people, and God used them mightily. That is until I read Isaiah 57:1-2, (NKJV) recently during my devotion time. "The righteous perishes, and no man takes it to heart. Merciful men are taken away, while no one considers that the righteous is taken away from evil, he shall enter into peace; they shall rest in their beds, each one walking in his uprightness." I had felt in my heart that when God took our son Jamie home four years ago, this was true of God's purpose in his death. He was very healthy, physically fit, until the rapid growing brain tumor he had hit him. I had read that verse many times I'm sure, but for some reason, it is like I read it for the first time. I just hadn't paid attention to it.

All of a sudden, I realized that was the reason God took so many devout men and women home. He spared good men from evil, so they could enter into peace and rest. They were like my son; he just cared too much about too many things going on in the world now. The fortunate ones are the ones God calls home. They were blessed by God. I was one of the ones that were left behind, but I do not feel sorry for them, for they are with God. How can it get any better than that? I do grieve over what is happening in our country today. What a world we live in. I often cringe when I hear the news. Yet, at the same time, I realize that more and more people are looking for hope. So, this gives us an open door to show them the only way to get it.

When there is death of a child, there is deep grief, especially to young parents. Even if those parents were Christians. Somehow, no one believes it could happen to them. When it does, their faith is shaken. Somehow, they have not learned the principle that every child is just loaned to us by the Lord and He has the right to take them home any time He wills. We actually are to merely raise them for Him and let Him do the rest. As hard as it is to accept, some children are simply born to die. Why? Only God knows. His ways are definitely not our ways. His thoughts are way past our understanding. That is where we have to cry out for His GRACE.

Sometimes, death to our child may just be caused by living in a sin-scarred world where the genes of our ancestors are passed down. Or the Lord simply knows the good He will work out of this child's death will be for His glory in the end. I often think of John Marsh, who lost a precious son who was kidnapped, abused, and later killed. He has devoted his life to finding missing children. How easy it would have been for him to just shake his fist at God and been bitter his whole life. The testimony of a parent to another person after their child has died is invaluable. I never went through such a tragedy, so how can I feel the emotions they feel. As caring as I am, I cannot do this. They want to know what others who have walked that dark, deep path, to share how they got out of that whole, and they, too, could finally climb out of theirs.

No death is a simple matter to anyone. But there is grace available for the one calling for it. I can share that for I have received such grace. The key, I guess, is not to keep our eyes on the tragedy, but on the Lord who can get us through it. All too often, people go to everyone but the One who can help them. When Corrie Ten Boom was told by her father that she would not be able to get through the death of loved ones except by grace, and it wasn't available until she needed it. When we need it, it will be there.

Only a person who experienced dying can testify of this, and I am one of them. I have never feared death, but I have to admit I did fear dying. You see, I had seen some dying, gasping for those last breaths and their pain and emaciated bodies. And I didn't like the thought of that happening to me. Oh, but that grace I had heard about was so real.

Suddenly, unexpectedly, what happened explains the whole experience. I realized I could no longer breathe, and hoarsely told the nurses. One quickly checked me and immediately issued a Code Blue. There just happened to be a surgeon on the ward, and skilled nurses who came running. All I could remember was I knew I was dying, no pain, no time, just this most awesome peace I ever experienced before. The next thing I remembered briefly was I was being rushed down a hall on a cart to surgery and heard some frantic people saying, "Hurry up, she is really bleeding." I had no time to do anything else before I went out again, except in my mind pray, "Well Lord, it looks like I'm coming home."

I woke up in recovery later and was told I had hemorrhaged due to a vein or artery that had come untied in my neck. What God taught me was He was sufficient, even in the process of dying. I did not see a long tunnel, a bright light, nor did I experience floating above my body and watching them working on me. Not that I will argue with anyone else's experience. That is not what this is about. All I know is what I experienced and what it taught me, for I believe with all my heart that is why He let this happen to me. God is faithful, and His grace is sufficient for all occasions. I will never fear dying again. And I know however it comes, there is *dying grace* available and I need not fret. Now that I am in my 80's, I realize why old people have said death was highly under-rated. It is the living long that is over-rated. It is like my husband used to say, "Living is what is killing him."

After my beloved husband died in total peace at home around his family, my grandchildren were told if they could use any of Papa's tools or other things stored in the garage, they could just agree and share them. While doing that, I found some poems I had written to them over thirty years ago in a manila envelope I had saved. My daughter-in-law told me I had written another one and given it to her when she had lost her baby girl at birth. I think it is worth printing. This is a time of great testing I know, but I only hope it can help a poor mother going through the same thing.

A babe was born one sun lit day,
But quickly that sun slipped away.
Conceived in love, and born the same,
Karen Elizabeth was her name.

Tucked in the arms of a mother's love,
Yet, bound to make her home above.
Just a moment, just a breath,
Then so quickly taken in death.

Mom, don't cry, please don't ache for me,
For here I am in God's arms you see.
Never a tear will touch my eye,
Never a need, nor cause to cry.

Never a day given over to sin,
I'm pure and spotless without, within.
No heartache, no grief, pain or despair,
That's just for earth children to bear.

Of all the children woman bear,
God chose your dear baby to spare.
Love so amazing, love so great,
This is your precious baby's fate.
Remember me, love me, but let your sun shine,
For all heaven's treasures now you see are mine.

Though this was the greatest test my youngest son and his wife went through, they know today that God has worked this adversity for the good for others from their experience. Please read the end chapters the Ultimate Test, and the Ultimate Release.

The Ultimate Test

The final days of one's life, or the final days of a mate, parent, child, or dear friend, can lead you to this ultimate test. Yes, I believe the ultimate test for all of us is death. Whether you pass this test or not, can depend on many variables, but one way or another, you cannot escape it. The only way, of course, is if you are blessed to live until the Rapture of the Church. I guess the only other way would be if you dropped dead unexpectedly. Then, the test would be passed on to others.

Jim, my husband, dealt with pain for several years. In the year before he passed, he endured, at times excruciating pain. I know now why. You see, the doctors had been treating him for the symptoms, and never did, until before he died, diagnose the disease that was causing him pain. I have to admit, I felt at times he just wouldn't accept the reality of having to live with pain. He persistently sought to find out why he had this pain from various doctors.

Included in that search was a trip to Phoenix, Arizona where he had been accepted by the Mayo Clinic for treatment. Jim couldn't seem to get that diagnosis anywhere else.

Jim went through a barrage of tests for a week and a half. To make a long story short, they found no surgery or other treatment would help him. One of the surgeons phoned him, and told him he strongly suspected that he had Multiple Myeloma and wanted him to be checked by his doctor as soon as he returned home. My husband, who was in pain, and didn't hear well, just never caught the seriousness of the matter, so he simply told me they couldn't help him. This was so disturbing to me.

When we returned home, Jim was put in the hospital with terrible pain, before he could see a doctor, due to it being a holiday. They discovered he had kidney stones and needed emergency surgery to open up a tube between kidney and bladder. It was performed, and Jim underwent some awful side effects from the anesthesia. One very sharp oncologist, not knowing a thing about Jim's history, ordered a bone marrow biopsy. He suspected, and it was confirmed, that he had a severe case of Multiple Myeloma. The pain had simply been a symptom of this disease. Upon going to our family doctor, we found the doctors from the Mayo Clinic had written him and told them they suspected this disease and requested tests.

Jim was immediately treated with chemo, as this is a treatable cancer of plasma cells in bones. Unfortunately, he had terrible reactions to this chemo, which put him back in the hospital. After realizing his old body couldn't take the chemo, and the pain was unbearable not to mention breathing problems and lesions on tongue and throat, he asked to go home and die. He never ate again, and could barely swallow water. Thanks to Hospice care, he was made comfortable and died less than two weeks later.

When you love someone as I loved Jim, I felt every pain he did. He had preached the gospel for years, loved people, and had a burning desire to see souls come to the Lord. I cannot tell you just how Satan buffeted me, with thoughts that my husband didn't deserve this. I am as committed as Jim was to the Lord, but I struggled every step of the way with what he had endured. One night, while Jim was in the hospital, the Lord spoke to me. He told me things I knew theoretically, but it was different with Jim. He told me He could've healed Jim anytime He chose to. This wasn't His plan. His thoughts or ways were not mine and past my understanding. He would accomplish what He planned, and what was required of me was to trust Him. (Isaiah 55:8-10, NKJV)This was not theoretical knowledge, this was practical knowledge. I cried, but I yielded to His way. When I visited Jim the next day was when he shared the decision he had made, to cease all treatments and go home to die. I simply told him I would support him in whatever decision he made. It was like he was just waiting for me to say that. He smiled and told the doctor what he was going to do and he actually was happy.

My testing actually began when I had to serve Jim, and had to do for him all the things he had done for me over sixty years. I even had to clean up beds multiple times, and carpet, clothes, and yes, even him. Love doesn't ever stop loving. But, I am not a server by nature. It was a new area to be travelled. Travelling to the hospital each day forty-five miles one way was not easy for a 78 year old woman. My boys came home and helped all they could, and I will forever be thankful for them. One lives in Virginia, and one in Arizona. But I must emphasize that ministering to Jim night and day for a week and a half, though an act of love, was not easy. Many tears were shed when I was alone. I didn't think, at times, I could make it another day. But, let me say, I learned how to trust God, and I can say HE IS SUFFICIENT. I hope Jim didn't have to endure all this so I could finish up this book. You see, one can never share anything that one hasn't learned himself. No matter what is asked of us, God's grace is there at our bidding. I can testify of that. Philippians 4:13, (NIV) is true.

Divorce is much like losing a loved one to death, for it is the death of a marriage. It is the ultimate betrayal. How many men or women have been divorced by their mate because of infidelity? More than we wish to talk about. It truly is an end of one's hopes, dreams, often financial security, lifestyle, sense of being loved, experiencing the joys of faithfulness, and protection. And when it happens, their life seems to fall apart, as well. After all, the one flesh principle is a great illustration of the fractured life they must now rebuild upon. One half of their body has been torn away and they are left emotionally bleeding.

This is one area I have never had to deal with, praise God. But, I have met so many women who have suffered this ultimate betrayal. Actually, some have shared with me it would have been easier on them if they had suffered the death of their mate. I live with knowing my husband is with the Lord, and has entered eternal bliss. This is quite different than knowing a husband who one assumed would be faithful until death left them, and were faced with the knowledge of their betrayal. This is even doubly painful if you still loved your mate or there were young children involved, who were innocent. Some children have thought they were in some way responsible for the break up. How can we estimate the tragedy, fractured lives of children due to broken homes?

Our Lord never wanted this to happen. That is why He has said so much about one man and one woman being faithful forever. I have always said before every commandment of God we should interject, "Because I love you." He gave these very commandments to protect us and provide the abundant life for us and our children. With the increase of divorce today, we have seen the increase of fractured lives. How sad! Is it any wonder we are told to return to the old ways, which are the good ways, Jeremiah 6:16, (NKJV). God's ways are best.

It is possible for God to restore a marriage. I do not want to leave that out. I have seen this several times in Jim's ministry. But, that depends on a person's repenting, and both parties being good forgivers and forgetters. I know of three such restorations. One was a pastor who actually left his wife, and his ministry, for another woman. His wife refused to believe God could not bring him back to her, and she told him so. She refused to believe he stopped loving her, and told him the affair was purely lust. After many years, he came back and asked her forgiveness and asked her to re-marry him. She did, and they had a more beautiful marriage than ever. God even convicted her of things she needed to change in her own life and it was a beautiful thing to see.

Another was in a situation where love had turned into hate. The man went to pick up his children weekly, and wasn't allowed to get out of his car, things were so tumultuous. He later was saved, prayed, and had the church pray also. One day, the girls didn't come out and run to his car when he arrived. Wondering what was wrong; he went to the door and knocked. His former wife, it seems, had a great conviction fall upon her and she told the girls to make him knock. She confessed how ugly she had been, and how ridiculous it was her forbidding the children to let him come to the door. He never left the house that day. She later was saved, and today, they have one of the happiest marriages possible. You say this cannot happen, oh, but it can in God's economy. I agree, not many have the faith that this man or the above woman had, but nothing is impossible with God. Jeremiah 32:27, "Behold, I am the Lord, the God of all flesh, is anything too hard for Me?" Never, no never.

The third example is of a devoted couple, both children of pastors who thought it would never happen to them. But it did. He had a fling with a former girlfriend, and at once, was convicted heavily. Both were crushed, once the ugliness was revealed. Restoration took place, and both became better, not bitter, and realized they, too, were vulnerable. He became a better husband, she a better wife, and testified that though this was something they wished no one would ever experience, they were more in love than before.

I know God didn't need this to make it what it became, but He used it to bring about the final result. Romans 8:28, (NKJV) is so true: "And we know that all things work together for good to those who love God, to those who are the called according to His purpose." They have both been able to help young couples who have experienced the same breach of their marriage vows. Forgiveness is far better than divorce.

The Ultimate Release

"We are confident, I say, and willing rather to be absent from the body, and to be present with the Lord." (2 Corinthians 5:8, KJV) That is the ultimate release. Up until then, we live in these physical bodies, which is our "earth suit" so to speak, with all its limitations, humiliations, afflictions, complications, imperfections, deficiencies, disabilities, perplexities, anxieties, uncertainties, etc. Surely, if a person has accepted Christ as their Savior, death releases them from all these things.

We do not always look at it this way, but truly, we will be blessed when we experience that release. Revelation 14:13, (KJV) says, "Then I heard a voice from heaven say, Write: 'Blessed are the dead who die in the Lord from now on.'" "Yes says the Spirit, that they may rest from their labors, and their works follow them." Yes, it will be a blessing to leave these old worn out bodies behind. We will be glad to get rid of this sinful, sick, weary body when that day comes.

When I was young, other than the childhood contagious diseases that go around, I was basically healthy. Having lived in a moral society, and having moral parents, I was better grounded than most today. I can honestly say I didn't have to cope with many of the temptations, as I was pretty secluded from the world. My first serious health problem didn't happen until I had thyroid cancer when sixty years old. It was detected early and had surgery, which cured the cancer. In my 70's, I had the common replacement of hips and a knee. Still, I managed to keep going like the Energizer bunny. Now that I am rapidly approaching my 80's and have lost both a son and husband to cancer that ravaged their otherwise healthy bodies, I am looking forward to that final release, death.

You see, I've had a glimpse of what lies ahead, and going home to be with the Lord is great gain. As Paul said in Philippians 1:21, (NIV), "For me to live is Christ, and to die is gain." I will gain freedom from all those aches, pains, sorrows, sufferings, and the problems of the world. I will gain freedom when I die in Christ; I am certain. Revelation 21:4, (KJV) says, "God Himself will wipe away every tear from their eyes. There will be no more death or mourning or crying or pain, the old order of things has passed away." I will gain sweet fellowship with my Lord. And I will gain fellowship with the saint of the ages. Oh, that will be glory to me!

Death is certain, unless we happen to be one of the blessed ones who will meet Christ in the air. Hebrews 9:27-28, (NIV) says, "Just as man is destined to die once, and after that to face judgment, so Christ was sacrificed once to take away the sins of many people; and he will appear a second time, not to bear sin, but to bring salvation to those who are waiting for him." At the Rapture of the church, all Christians will be caught up in the air, not having to go through death. Since that is so, the ultimate release shouldn't be something to fear, but to be ready for, and to look forward to. I'm not talking about fatalism, but an honest preparation for the inevitable.

There is only one way to prepare for this ultimate release. That is through faith in the Lord Jesus Christ. There is no other way. Look at Ephesians 2:8-9, (KJV, emphasis): "For by grace (gift of God) you have been saved through faith, (a deep heart belief in God's provision for us), and that not of yourselves, (Jesus paid the price in full for us by dying on the cross in our place,) it is the gift of God, not of works, (anything we could do to earn it, that would be wages not a gift), lest anyone should boast."

He who believes in the Son, (that He took our condemnation), has everlasting life, (eternal life) and He who does not believe (faith), the Son shall not see life, but the wrath of God (judgment) abides in him. In John 3:36 (emphasis), Jesus said to them, "I am the (only) way, the (only) truth, the (only) life. No one comes to the Father (God), except through me."

There is only one way to prepare for this ultimate release. To believe Jesus is the only way and to accept this great gift given to us by God. He stands today with open arms. Matthew 11:28, (NKJV) says, "Come unto Me, all you who labor and are heavy laden, and I will give you rest." The promise of this verse is that in this physical life also, with all its turbulence, we can still have rest. And the last part of Revelation 14:13b, (NKJV) says, "Yes says the Spirit, that they may rest (perfect) from their labors, and their works do follow them." Oh, what joy knowing that our labors in Christ's name have not been in vain.

What a perfect release, from laboring to rest. The knowledge, that our works done in love, and from our hearts, will be rewarded, though few have appreciated our work. John 8:36, (NKJV) says, "Therefore if the Son makes you free, you shall be free indeed." Death is the ultimate release and it means ultimate freedom. Free at last!

Having seen death of non-Christians, Christians, loved ones and knowing at best, I cannot have too many years, I can tell you that death has no sting to me. I am ready anytime the Lord feels my work here is done. I am not trying to rush it by any means, but am ready anytime the Lord is. I look forward to the ultimate release I will have at that time.

Until Then,
Trust & Obey

This is the marching orders of a Christian. So often, we don't know what we are to do in any given situation we face. When this happens, a still small voice tells us we must simply trust and obey. All of us are familiar with the song: "Trust and Obey"[8], written by John H. Sammis and the tune written by Daniel B. Towner. The chorus says, "Trust and obey, for there's no other way to be happy in Jesus, but to trust and obey."

When writing this book, God would wake me during the night, by my hearing a phone ring. But when I awoke, my phone, which is by my bed, would not be ringing. At first, I thought it was only my imagination, but I eventually realized it was the Lord's way of waking me up to write. Words, songs, or Bible verses would pop into my head, and I would write down whatever I heard. What was required of me was to *simply* trust and obey.

It takes a great deal of trust to do what the Lord commands, for it often makes no sense at all. And why should that surprise me. God's ways never make sense at first, but when we *simply* trust and obey, then and only then, will we see the why of the matter.

---

[8] Sammis, John H. and Towner, Daniel B. "Trust and Obey". (1887)

I have wondered *why me* when the Lord told me to write this book. There are so many Christian writers, authors, who certainly could do so much better than I can, for they are much more capable than I am. I have, *simply put*, just trusted God and obeyed His command. I pray that God, who told me to *simply* trust and obey Him, can use this book to do what He intended all along.

As I look back at my life, I now realize it can be summed up in these two words, trust and obey. I am certain that the time left for me in this life, however many years that will be, will also be the same. One thing I can testify to is, when I have trusted and obeyed, He has been faithful in whatever He asked of me. To God be all the glory.

Psalm 34:8, (NKJV) says, "Oh taste and see that the Lord is good; Blessed is the man who trusts in Him!" 1 Peter 4:17, (NKJV) says, "For the time has come for judgment to begin at the house of God; and if it begins with us first, what will be the end of those who do not obey the gospel of God?" Before I go home and be with the Lord, I am sure that there will be many more times I will have to be reminded of this simple command, to trust and obey.

What does the future hold for me? I have no idea, and certainly don't know how much will be required of me in this area. I just pray that I will be as faithful as my Lord and Savior has been to me. May God bless you.

About the Author

Theresa J. Royal was born and reared in Willimansett, Massachusetts. She graduated from Chicopee High School where she took Secretary training. "Terri," as she is affectionately known, met and married her husband Jim who was in the Air Force, and became a beautician. After her husband retired from the Air Force, she became a pastor's wife for 24 years. Both she and her husband did voluntary mission work for eleven years in Kino Bay, Sonora, Mexico. Terri has spent forty years teaching, and still teaches Ladies' Bible studies.

www.ingramcontent.com/pod-product-compliance
Lightning Source LLC
Chambersburg PA
CBHW070020100426

42740CB00013B/2566